*Judith Rodriguez*
NEW AND SELECTED POEMS

Judith Rodriguez was born in Perth and brought up in Brisbane. A graduate of the universities of Queensland and Cambridge, she has taught literature at universities and colleges in Jamaica, London and Australia, and has conducted many writing courses. She now lectures in Writing and Literature at Deakin University. Judith Rodriguez's linocut prints have appeared in books, journals and exhibitions. She has edited *Mrs Noah and the Minoan Queen* an anthology of one generation of Australian women poets, and the *Collected Poems* of Jennifer Rankin. She is collaborating as librettist with composer Moya Henderson, on the opera *Lindy*, commissioned by the Australian Opera.

**By the same author:**

*Verse*
"A question of ignorance" in Four Poets
Nu-plastik Fanfare Red
Water Life
Shadow on Glass
Mudcrab at Gambaro's
Witch Heart
Floridian Poems

*As editor*
Mrs Noah and the Minoan Queen
Poems Selected from the *Australian's* 20th Anniversary
Competition (with Andrew Taylor)

*Art Text*
Noela Hjorth (with Vicki Pauli)

# Judith Rodriguez
## NEW AND SELECTED POEMS

# The House by Water

University of Queensland Press
ST LUCIA • LONDON • NEW YORK

First published 1988 by University of Queensland Press
Box 42, St Lucia, Queensland 4067 Australia
Reprinted 1992

Poems and linocuts © Judith Rodriguez 1962, 1973, 1976, 1978, 1980, 1982, 1986, 1988, 1992

This book is copyright. Apart from any fair dealing
for the purposes of private study, research, criticism
or review, as permitted under the Copyright Act, no
part may be reproduced by any process without written
permission. Enquiries should be made to the publisher.

Typeset by University of Queensland Press
Printed in Australia by The Book Printer, Victoria

Distributed in the USA and Canada by
International Specialized Book Services, Inc.,
5602 N.E. Hassalo Street, Portland, Oregon 97213-3640


**Cataloguing in Publication Data**
*National Library of Australia*

Rodriguez, Judith, 1936-
   The house by water : new and selected poems / Judith Rodriguez.
   p.  cm. — [UQP paperbacks]

   I. Title.

PR9619.3.R6H68  1988  821 — dc19  88-17607

ISBN 0 7022 2138 4 [pbk.]

On a day of few shadows
dark and light as cloud
the house by water
still as a bird
listens

till people
come driving their kids
along the dirt road
all sat among stacks of coke-cans
and raucous in yellow water-wings.

"The House by Water"
from *Witch Heart*

# Contents

Acknowledgments   *xiv*

## The Mahogany Ship (1975-1984)

Lake season   *2*
Early to the lake   *3*
At the bottom   *4*
Presentation   *5*
Measuring up   *6*
The search for fulfilment   *7*
The ten-metre board   *8*
Poolfish   *10*
The case wrapped up   *11*
Lake evening   *12*
Lake valley   *14*
A late view; Schloss Esterhazy   *16*
The lake isle of Werribee: a fable   *17*
Torrens '82   *19*
The surf tank   *20*
Beach lagoon   *21*
Sea-litany   *22*
Waves by night   *23*
Figures on the horizon   *24*
Galilee   *25*
Wreck
    I   *The captain of the ill-fated ship returns*   *26*
    II  *The criminals are taken to the island*   *27*
    III *The condemned men account for their actions*   *27*
    IV *To show righteousness exists*   *28*
    V  *They ask that their leader be executed first*   *29*

On steering a course  *30*
Bass writes, February 1803  *31*
Beyond Belmont  *33*
The mahogany ship  *35*

**The White Room (1982–1986)**

The white room  *38*
Practising incapacity  *39*
The night rumour  *40*
Night talk  *41*
Crow notes  *42*
A way with birds  *43*
Passing the island  *44*
The rat-king  *45*
At home, beloved  *46*
The bird of night  *47*
The end of the lift  *48*
Getting back from the outing  *49*
Day with one cloud  *50*
In-flight note  *51*
All that carolling about the Christ child  *52*
Mentors  *53*
Answer to Why?  *54*
The journey with children  *55*
The letter from America  *56*
The late lemon tree  *58*
Face for casting  *59*
The address  *60*
Potato-field at Ampton  *61*
To the city visitors . . .  *63*
Five poems on memory  *65*
Bagged giraffe  *67*
An old bag, printed "Cynthia"  *68*
The emperor  *69*

**Floridian Poems (1986)**

Wild shiners  *72*

Zouave marching team, Rollins College, 1913–1914    73
TV sacrament    74
The day the world turned over    75
A meeting in Winter Park    77
Re-routed in the States    78
Bear dream    79
Condominium poems
    *Adult mobile homes*    80
    *No more worries*    82
    *Viewing at the condominium*    84
    *The Bolivian lady*    85
Dream houses    87

**Poems 1960–1972**
*including poems from* Four Poets *and* Nu-plastik Fanfare Red

The bush-fiddle    90
The intellectual traveller    92
Horses to the sea: a Romantic motif    95
For Hazim Abdullah    96
My grandmother
    *My grandmother retraces evolutionary paths*    97
    *Her village*    97
    *She speaks*    98
Aussie returns, 1969    100
Getting home    102
Nu-plastik fanfare red    103
Drums in the suburb    105
Afternoon suburb, framed by kitchen    107
Black and white, mostly white    108
Talking of people    110
Open-air cinema    112
June 1970    113
Nothing a child does    114
Centipede    115
Verandahs
    *Eighties pub*    116
    *Sunflowers in iron*    116
    *Dream-watch*    117

Sunday outing  *119*
Sojourners at Phoenix  *120*

**Water Life (1972–1975)**

About this woman  *124*
Rebeca in a mirror  *125*
The scissors  *127*
Polar  *128*
Charm: to receive a letter  *129*
Lying late Sunday morning  *130*
Flower-poem  *132*
At the nature-strip  *133*
Occasion for elegy  *134*
The questioner in black  *135*
A lifetime devoted to literature  *136*
In the vanguard  *137*
Report to the Anthropology Center  *138*
How come the truck-loads?  *139*
Towards fog  *140*
Reconnaissance  *142*
Changing the subject  *143*
Jellyfish  *144*
Bivalve  *145*
Manatee  *147*
Poems drowning  *149*
Poems fished out  *150*
Eskimo occasion  *151*
Water a thousand feet deep  *152*
Penelope at Sparta  *153*
Borges at 73  *155*
Water life  *158*

**Shadow on Glass (1974–1978)**

A photo of me in which I do not appear  *162*
The night  *163*
Now I start to print  *163*
Kin  *164*

The double    *164*
Epigram    *165*
The daily round    *165*
Wife alone    *166*
At the corner of my eye    *167*
Sequence    *168*
Á la carte    *168*
After    *169*
All OK?    *169*
The eye swims    *170*
Carrying a candle    *170*
Body and soul    *171*
Exit the lamplighter    *172*
Game    *173*
A shadow cast on glass    *173*

## Mudcrab at Gambaro's (1976–1979)

Legends of the Nevado    *176*
Family    *178*
Old friends    *179*
Writing a biography    *180*
The piano on the beach    *181*
Palais de danse    *182*
The big girl    *184*
I've always wanted a brass dodo    *185*
And behold, it was very good    *186*
Cooker for the rubbish-tip    *187*
Clearing a cupboard    *188*
The line of tearing    *189*
Is it poetry? they ask.    *190*
A line of notes    *191*
An odd voyage    *192*
Isadora    *195*
Madrigal    *196*
Replay    *197*
Soldier's gravestone, Kalemegdan    *198*
Tutorial    *199*

Mudcrab at Gambaro's
> *Mudcrab at Gambaro's*    200
> *The subject*    201
> *An upbringing*    202
> *Occasions of mudcrab*    204
> *The mudcrab-eaters*    206
> *On going for mudcrab*    206

Fourteen times saying rain for Tom    208
The line always there    210

## Witch Heart (1979-1982)

How do you know it's the right one?    212
Leaving    213
Leaving the trees    214
Travelling    215
That house of yours    216
Homecoming    217
The waking    219
A concerned aerial view    220
The surprise    221
Arms race    222
Drew    224
Canoes    225
The city workers    226
A legal error, 29th March, 1847    227
Wintering inland    228
Laughter in fall    229
The glove    231
Strop    232
Dinner at River Acres    233
Funny    234
The night hand    235
Halley's Comet    236
Witch heart    237

## Nasturtia! (1978-1982)

A bed of nasturtiums    240
Nasturtium grows    241

Her lookout  *241*
Prophetic nasturtium  *242*
Epic nasturtium  *242*
Emblem  *243*
Wanton  *243*
Nasturtium no student  *244*
The rising generation  *244*
Nasturtium watches the cyclists  *245*
Nasturtium untanned  *245*
Nasturtium regardless  *246*
Her company  *246*
Showdown  *247*
Viewing  *247*
Hardy nasturtium  *248*
The confirmation  *248*
Fat in winter  *249*
The long hot summer  *249*
No question  *250*
One and Many  *250*
One night  *251*
Nasturtium scanned  *251*
Naming Nasturtium  *252*

# Acknowledgments

Acknowledgment is made to the following, in which previously uncollected poems first appeared: the *Age*, *Antipodes* (USA), *Ariel*, *Artisan*, *Artlook*, *Arts National*, *Aspect*, the *Australian*, the *Bulletin Literary Supplement*, *Compass*, *Don Quichotte*, *Fling! Image*, *Luna*, *The Malahat Review*, *Meanjin*, *New Poetry*, *Northern Light*, *Overland*, *Poetry Australia*, *Radio Waves*, *Southerly*, the *Sydney Morning Herald*, *Tasmanian Review*, *This Australia*, *Turnstile*, *Waves*, *West Coast Review* and *Radio 5UV; Lines from the Horizon*, edited by Christopher Pollnitz; *The Penguin Book of Australian Women Poets*, edited by Susan Hampton and Kate Llewellyn; *Australian Poetry 1986*, edited by Vivian Smith.

This book would not exist without writer's fellowships (1974, 1978 and 1983) from the Literature Board of the Australia Council) and its sponsorship of a writer-in-residency at Rollins College, Florida. Particular gratitude is due also to Rollins College for this time to write and for its generosity in printing a limited edition of *Floridian Poems*.

# The Mahogany Ship

1975–1984

*The cup at David's*

# Lake season
*for Tom*

Because of the impossibility
that I should know your years, and you mine,
and though we did not find
our children together
in the first garden —

on Toronto island spring comes
and the squatters in beach cottages
dance in the lake-dawns
and civic favour,
and Marian dances,

by Lake Balaton
winter reed-cutting is over,
under the mountain trees glow,
the boar rushes out,
the new antlers jostle —

these to our valley
of hanging gardens
assailed by the wrecker with new plans
we bring, a vision of lakes,
a second fruiting.

# Early to the lake

I go down to the lake.
Mist has claimed its shore.
The dark mud, bearings –
behind, where I came from,
the thin trees of the slope
would each near suddenly
then move back. Now they are gone.

I came early, alone.
And it is truly the world's egg.
I call, and the pulse
heading out, stops –
The mist gives back nothing.
The lake spreads in me.
I am in time for the beginning.

# At the bottom

Here lies
one eye in mud

the other tries scanning up
pit-sides

something shining
dims

which is it clouding over

thinks of that other someone
hanging on

giving one eye the run of it all
right from the beginning

believing at least it must be there
the way in

turning a blind eye

## Presentation

Thought often of degutting.
What you do first with fish.

Go in after it. Know where to cut.
Have it all out.

The rest, so clean, neatened off.
Mysterious ends.

Get it on a tray for godsake.
Fold if you know packaging.

The edge hanging clear all round.
What a spread to wheel out.

But it had to all end there.
This toting round flesh.

## Measuring up

Your rising suburban sales manager
lies on water
he is relaxing his image
and will probably instal heating.

One day last week
to an associate
he mentioned waterbeds –

the Board queried

was he currently feeling
quite fit?
had his leave accrued?

Changing direction on his li-lo
he can still see his toes
the trend's slow coming and Christ
only walked on water.

# The search for fulfilment:

                                      this common
ant at a reasonable venture
starts up the side of a saucepan
containing water.

Providence leans, does her hand's-turn —
puts the pot on the hot-plate:

ant gets hot feet, faster,
tries out, there's this hellish gale
upward, tries in, oceans,
wants speed, wants wings, wants.
A fingertip half on singe dips,
passes, flicks again. Outside
reason preserved, the frantic
ant tracks.

# The ten-metre board

Dared
by no-one
but myself

climbed the steep rungs
to the three-metre
then higher

visible but not too purposed
pitched to the act
but not to intending it

the grip grip of ascending
my private fanfare
countdown

and then on the rope-knotty footing
not wet with use to the end
by stage-steps

and the baths coming up all vertical   the
    swimmers' lane-markings
stilled
as never from the restless sides or the big-stepped seats

and the moment
the exemplary smash closer
than the board one step behind

did it    dived    down through water's instant
to push away concrete    crawl it forcibly
the minute scorings    paint lifting at hairlines

while buoyancy and lungs remembered
each other
and strained to each     nearly     nearly

till the meeting
thrashed but I'd done it
and could casually tell everyone

At thirteen
there was life in that
I didn't need to do it again

now I'd line up the finer points
approach     exercise of the board's dormant tensions
wakening a line of flight

flying into fall
re-entry     the dead-stop coursing
and the half-death in air

and beyond
never to be told
beyond even the slammed concrete

time and again
keeping the life in it keeping it
an event

# Poolfish

Risen between walls, by me
water remembers its bed
breeding among stones and mud.

I too have memories
past the deceit
of blue paint and sachets.

I breathe chlorine,
Weedo and Thrive.
I co-exist with grass-cuttings.

My gills pulse on
through stark interventions
of 500 watts

when deity by night
bursts in and down —
sun-spawn!

I too have ideas
of progress, the return
beyond plastic fronds.

Three generations from now
I may have created mud
and I expect to have a godlike body.

## The case wrapped up

In the rippled pool
I thought I had left it behind:
clutter. And the growing.

First they threw in the pot-plants.
Then the backyard grill, with sausages
that inched up, trailing.

Down, probing, came
the 500-watt pool lamp
through a lace spread of insects.

The interrogation
began under a spate of planking
and pool furniture,

Exhibit A
was the wiring. Such a case to answer!
But I didn't jump bail

till the railing sprouted —
next thing, they'd programme chlorine
resentments to follow me.

# Lake evening

After the cool bright day, the boat-party, the laughter,
    they pause
scattered above the lake, for this:
the falling still.

Singular jewel!
Deepening beyond wish – transparence blue as day's ideal –
resides the echo, ghost of rhyme.

Unmatched, a spark in the firmament veers
and teeters, snaps off. A lustrous whim
obscurely moves in the lake,

there wells up
the offshore nightwind, backsurge
jostles the tethered rank of switch-on boats and
    clatters pier-planks,

a flutter of white-lacquered straw
mounts out of the swagged vines on the last unshadowed slope
round to the terrace.

But nobody has come yet. They are trying on bowties
    and rings
in rooms, guessing the service-charge.
Shadow draws on, becomes one,

becomes many, there is a pulse in the enclosed lake,
    exhalations, whisperings,
engine-tone breaks near the far shore
and the beacon cross

on its whitewashed plinth slams centre in a race of headlights
then drowns again. Already sated
they are ordering on the brilliant terrace.

At the turn way over
undersides of fog prepare a glimmering seige.
The iron lappings, the hard winter.

# Lake valley

Everything in the valley tumbles in:
rings worn on boat-trips — snow —
all the best farming land has worked down there too.

The people of the lake churchyard are entranced in a slow
dive; plinth and rail follow; they glide
from beds of conception to the miles and miles of lake-bed

weed, fleshed for water, downward-mouthing at mud.
All of it in a waver, the whorl
of each sky-change impressed, fallen in with lake purposes,

however clouds whisk away. Nothing's of the surface
only, nothing once lake can be lost,
it all comes to new life in the mountain valley's wound;

drought can only plaster it awhile, and the divers won't find
the depth of it. What tourists throw in —
lunch-wraps, the good-luck coin from a stopover — inhabits

less than their faces, heavy with water, cross-hatched
with dark-pink pulsing weed
and greasy-stroked light from the listing boat's ripples . . .

A conqueror might breast the pass and note his bauble:
lake-village. The valley's process
has been bagged, a month's knee-scraped scrambling, in a
    knapsack of specimens.

But the lake-alive, its veiny burrowing and branching, runs
in the farm-mother's rock-perched zany
come down shouting, a world of him, for the girl that makes
    beds at the inn.

# A late view, Schloss Esterhazy

At Eisenstadt, harvest gathers. The courtyard stinks
of grapes in the press, afternoon
shadows grotesque heads, provincial mouldings.
Storeroom doors at-ease, no-one
is bothering with tourists from Vienna, who hang about
the entry — sniff the off-bounds basement —
with brochure-clamped fingers indicate, then snap light
wedged in a third-floor scroll or melting face —
and trail out unled, conclusionless, still marking the place.

Medallions of Magyar heroes stud the facade,
crimson on pear-yellow; Esterhazy
faces the Germanies (Vienna one day's ride) —
guardian of eastward marches
to vast Hungary, prince whatever Emperor visits
or tourist, gone to pace autumn in the park —
conservatories closed, walks sogged, ruined cottages
by the terrace, slopes of a golden clearing . . . Lake
shores stroll by the lodge, half-turn to eye the camera. Take!

# The lake isle of Werribee: a fable

Mary Matilda to Percy: "Percy, let's you and me
a snug grotto build us, of rock and sea-shell made —
it will be just like The Tempest! While Pa builds Werribee,
we'll play the mage and the sea-girt maid."

Percy to Mary Matilda: "Course we could, but what stuff:
it's miles to the surf-loud sea, rocks are an awful load,
you'll have to plant things to hold 'em, the shells will
    just fall off,
it'll end a mess — and it won't be okayed."

Mother to Mary Matilda: "Darling, I'll speak to Pa.
How clever of Percy to plan it, of course we must have a lake!
Pine and palm shall we plant there; once Webley's done
    with the ha-ha
he'll run in pipes while the stones are laid."

Mother to Father: "Andrew, approve the children's notion;
they want to do it themselves, the thing has no taint of trade,
their isle is a pretty feature, a garden lake's not an ocean,
they'll thank their Pa as we dine in state."

Father said, "Mary, I never refused the children in reason."
He added a rustic drawbridge to lower when the dinner-bell
    bade.
A plasterer mixed the plaster, they went to Webley for
    trees and
earth was carted and bills were paid.

"Percy," said Mary Matilda, "I'm glad I collected the shells."
She sat in her maiden's grotto and patterned and plastered
    and played.
Percy was edging back along the path from the cell's
grey mouth — he was off for guns and a ride —

and Percy came back with a bride. But Mary Matilda was
   gone;
the isle was shrubbery and vines, and the cavern walls inlaid
with knuckle-bones, cowries and cones; the lake never held
   water for long.
You pay to stroll the bunya'd glade.

# Torrens '82

Here we are on a pedal-boat, Festival of '82.
It has taken me three festivals to get as far as Jolley's
    Boathouse
with a willing partner pedaller sound of limb.

Up and down we go, legs threshing, knees bunching.
The lovers on the bank are undulating their necks, dipping
thoughtfully, mouth over juicy mouth, like the less sudden
    water-birds.
They are leaving the hip-stuff, the saucy tails, to the
    moorhens –
and the deep plunge, coming up somewhere else.

Decorum is in, these partnerships! He even passes me
the little handle, the tiller. Wanting not to be selfish.
And we turn in a wide curve below the mural on Festival
    Hall.
Upstream is easy as downstream. Wrong, he tells me,
    upstream
is downstream, indeed they feel the same, yes, just the
    same . . .
the Torrens is a lake, dammed. We are going nowhere.

We're a scribble in one plane, returning to mooring-point A,
enjoy the trip. By regulation. Suddenly where's the point?
We work, and head for shore.

# The surf tank

This is the tank of water and sand
rigged to show
how ocean makes its thundering obeisance
shallowing towards land.

On the left, shutters that circle and pretend
to be the very pulse
of immensity, with their mechanised shoving
of waves to the other end,

then the swell getting up, spurred on to rakish
linked curlicues
of a dado or watery architrave
ramping inshore to break

in a pother of spurts and bubbles, and that's
our demonstration –
just where on the inconstant shelving
ocean's edge devotes

its creatures to the ebb, or ruinous or airy
change, all change
from there on. Unrolling and overlapping
petals of seafoam vary

millionfold, still we recross the beach
into breakers, leap
to the massed one mothering rhythm
out of depths out of reach.

# Beach lagoon

They have drained the lagoon. For our good
where our sewage fouls the stream
Flinders' men provisioned at,
and the beach sand held it,

the council tractor ploughed a channel.
Seven dead toads, bloated
and gesturing, whisked out to ocean.
Wind scours the fetid

ditch drained to brown scum, toad-spawn
taped between grass-tufts, lost rings,
plastic lids, chunks of surf-board.
Moon-set, then new tide,

kids bring down nets, spear shallows
for tiddlers and trevally in a bucket.
Moon back at dawn, and high water,
sea-waves will enter –

sludged with a life's mixed seepage
mind burrows warm behind
the sandbar, fine-silts its broken shells,
thinks Pacific.

## Sea-litany

The sea throws itself on the sand.
These shreds of being.

The sea lays its spine on the sand.
Hauls it back.

The sea rocks its ribs on the sand.
Draws them back.

The sea gropes with hands on the shore.
Palms upward.

The sea flings its hair on the sand.
Desperate.

The sea floods
up a wind-cold shell-grit dune.
The sea winces.

The sea crowds its silvered children back and forth
under the moon.

The sea wastes on the day's sand.

The sea lays seige and appeases.

# Waves by night

I walk the room by night
the cards of fate are stacked on the ceiling
I walk the watery and the burnished shadows
among dark shapes and the heads of doorways

on the shore the waves beat
no pattern to their returnng

I walk the cells of my flesh
the loyal and the fickle do not declare themselves
my lover says I'll live to eighty-five
on the odds I can laugh at that     and I do

on the shore     waves
no pattern

I walk my life by half-light
my children hand me mirrors I weep to see
someone keeps parking right across my door
the wardrobe's overgrown the shores pile up

daylight over apartment roofs
like waves

# Figures on the horizon

In the morning they went off up the beach, our things
    in their arms –
sandals, towels, lollies wrapped in paper. They untied
    their shoes.
They built the mound, and shouted over waves' hushing:
There it was. They'd be back. And walked away with the dog.

Mist lifted, cloud thinned, sand dried. None of us bothered
following. But we half-saw, half-felt how she swung her red
    wedgies
by the thin red heel-straps she liked, with little gold buckles.
He had along a book. They never once looked back.

How it was, diminished into the great scene: that dog! she
    went mad,
printing the sands like a saw-blade, her ancestral imagination
herding walkers they met, dash and turn, cutting out
then pressing the straggler – only groups on the move found
    proper –

then her hip-hefting trot, to inspect banked rags of seaweed,
dash again. He and she walked barefoot, stood, straddled
    pools, bent,
took up their day to look at. Seas ran, shallows drained, dunes
fell back into haze. And the turn far along, the river-mouth.

In the afternoon they came and beckoned by the clothes full
    of blown sand
we'd never once made for. Trailing lobed frills, globules of
    sea-flesh,
shell-bits to pick over. Water greyed, held its detail, till the
    crew of us
towelling, that day-alone of growing-up, tossed round chatter.

# Galilee

Walking on water he was happier
finding in his father's womb
waters that did not break,
leaning to the planetary heart-beat
boatmen allow for,
felt on shore and far up
rivers, in rain and in
contrary weathers and terrains.

Walking, he turned and they saw
the terrible happiness in him
and Come, he said, for a moment
needing them, dear sharers,
the sun-blind faces.
But it dimmed and the water-crests
caught and twisted. He knew then
he was on his own, always.

# Wreck

I
*The captain of the ill-fated ship returns with help*
*for his ship's company set ashore on the island.*
*A massacre has occurred. The mutiny is put down and*
*the mutineers are punished.*

Southward, wary of the coast's silence and savage
islands and shoals, runs hope, near their hundredth day
of bird-cries, nights crouched against the south-west swell.
From hungry inlets, unprofitable tribesmen watch
us, men of substance, venture back into the trap
we fed once; according to oath; good faith under sail.
I practise the holy order of navigation,
salvation by laws and instruments. Our people's trust
pilots us true, tó them, company of castaways
at their three-month outpost; God's new word on these rocks,
where years from now a cup, a shoe, a sword-hilt
may make some chieftain great, his mate a belle,
give the pack a Christian fetish.
                                        . . . But the devil's wish with it,
terror! cutting of throats on the outcrop, six-score
thrown to the sea's teeth or plastered down with sand,
true light lost, and the lost left, stowed with the ship,
never to wear new cloth more or talk good Dutch,
walk carpet again, fill doorways . . .
                                        Justice was easy.
Not one of those hand-cropped hanged men visits my dreams.
Only, the island our keel chose, I had thought
marked out for blessings, eyes me like a plate
set for the sun to eat from. Over it they run
pincered, no good is left, they eat each other.

II
*The criminals are taken to the island,*
*tortured and executed.*

These who draw life no longer
in images of honour
                    howl

no knowledge
offering
      but hell

endlessly with rope and blade
they make and are made
                    howling

all they denied
and did


III
*The condemned men account for their actions.*


We had known crime – unbelievable injustice:
a routine trip, ship lost, the firmament shattered.
The messengers to the Company sailed with promises north.
Before many days we denounced the lack of faith
and looked for God's proofs and promise, there on the beach.
The drowned ship's wound groaned at us from the shambles
fathoms down, an age away, dead of her sin.
She had killed herself, outcast from God's grace, casting us
on a demonish quarter, fires burning inland
and tales of lost ships' people reaming our skulls.

## IV

To show righteousness exists
away from the Syndics' offices:
Cornelius said he would, and did,
the man found by the conditions.
*We had to live.*

O least believable blessing,
dimension here, of the possible:
mercy through this justice —
*to kill, and live.*

Lopping and harrying sin
with daily riddance and discipline,
we grew to it, became Him.
For our own evil-doing
most vigilant and strict,
killing without question or guilt;
and fear out of sight like the ship,
ballasted with Cornelius' justice;

*and so we live.*
If we have been remiss
the Syndics will give credit
to our need, to the difficulty,
to our intentions . . .

## V

*They ask that their leader be executed first*
*"that their eyes might see that the seducer of men died".*

Recalled, I die from this moment
incorruptibly;

air, diet, allegiance
all foreign,

life among tolerance and temporisers
unthinkable. They agree.

I follow discipline, my executioner
my convert, knowing it

the disease so strong for life
you die to put paid to it.

My fertile matter swims, each cell
opportunity for evil.

Toxins, defoliants, steroids —
to end, end somewhere

Him first, procurer and principal
who imagines me,

in the flesh this once finally
"that my eyes may see
   that the seducer of men dies"

— then kill light, let
me like salt silt

be lost among islets thought
never childs more

## On steering a course

Dinghy in the wake?
Rather be Bligh
a hundred days out –
his thronging breadfruit
tubs slithered down
past sweep of tides
feeding diluvian
scales in darkness,
and the Bounty gone
shipped over the edge
towards another
dimension – Pitcairn –

rather be Bligh
ridiculous, intent
on a daily ration
(ounces per day),
on lawful revenge
(cat and rope)
and of course, advancement
(spyglass and sextant
and Sydney Town
traduced by rum-rich
nabob-larrikins
twenty years hence).

# Bass writes, February 1803

Dear Bess, high summer here, and parched, not green.
Out from great gates of rock I'll show you some day
we sail for mountainous west coasts bearing secrets,
all excellently practical, like the little fires
the dusky maidens of our great south land
cook over in their forest — thin smoke's climbing —
for hunters. Ah! better than snakes and rats
we'll have for ourselves soon in Port Jackson town,
What do you say to pork — no, always full-stocked
when that's what I'm shipping, never mind, what do you say
to a fortune in reales and doubloons
and Spanish laces, goldwork, coloured shawls —
all traded for a little salvaged iron
Cook won't begrudge me, and other things, no need to tell
anyone, or how far east, but Henry knows.
One thing's no secret, Venus at our prow,
you, Bess! already queening it on this ocean
that smiles for a Venus. James Cook, who watched his pass
darkening the sun, thirty years back and more,
within a month vouchsafes me solid anchors
shall sell to sail mine half across the world
to her own snug Olympus. Neptune's favour!
You see, Bess, how I plan, how daring serves,
no mere barrel-pork this time for our lieutenants.
I've fish in view — near the iron — and grain and seeds
and beef and cattle too — from you don't know where.
And trinkets to please condesas and infantas!
Poor Matthew's sailing solemnly around
our desert land, or lands — but we saw the best
five years ago — taking soundings, drawing capes.
They pay him, and of course he'll use his eyes
but I doubt he'll find a single Spanish dollar.
No Venuses for him at this rate, love!

Ah, Bess, trust me, this voyage safely done,
a little clever signalling off the coasts,
running up into coves and river-mouths
under the tight Dons' noses . . . would I could
take off their sweltering slaves of Englishmen!
but we'll have their goods — Drake's must have been a day —
and home I'll come and twit your head-shaking father,
go shares with Bishop and Henry, and I'll snatch you up
and bring you back, dear Bess! — Weather outside, they say,
a wild sea this, but one I know too well,
dark Circes and storms, to fear or turn from. East
of the Andes I've not yet seen, beyond their crossroads
virgins and queenly Incas, your face, I kiss it,
snows . . .

# Beyond Belmont

Concede the Mutiny. Forget. The wind off the Strait
confirms trees in their bent, keeps acres low,
hushes the consequence of up-country authority
in a halfway-made officer advanced from the Rifles
and able, then, to ship out his Anne. Who viewed
his India shuddering righteous and blood-slobbered to duty,
and wide-eyed from women's talk, persuasive with horror
sold him to this countryside of maybe pasture
under the westerly, blonding in summer drought,
saltpans to the east and a savouring, always, toward sea.

She knew it, simply, for home. There was enough.
The scrub crouched, sketching humility beyond
their square of young pines. The headlands ran from gales
relinquishing wrecks. Unclimbable rock — soft
as tallow — cliffed round one point, layers sharp as linen
tumbled, another. The peninsula's uncleared lots
spread patient as an old one-coloured quilt.

Days of high zest, trees flowering yellow on blue
or the girls trying on for dances out Hamilton way,
woke his wound, the memory of ambition. Splendours
of India run to Empire rankled. Yet he hardly spoke,
his souvenirs, meditated but unstoried, came to rest
in his daughters' homes, and all his word that prevailed
was an opinion on the placing of the guns at Queenscliff
and a name — the house that burned after, and the
    made carriage-road
straight as a lance to the highway. Its rise you drive now
offers a new husk, wild-hedged stare-windowed concrete,
and prospect, grit-dark sunflowers huge with seed.
His tread's gone, and his horse, and the sheep he disliked,
    and his mind
to see Eastern markets and palaces again

if only for embroidered belts for the girls. This sign's
his time up towards Benares, a brief posting;
his feeling for the River, destiny of travelling men,
pinched to an alien clove among casuarinas.
Here. Spicing antarctic air, the land
of cave-keeping castaways and shepherds, a winter's space,
your sea-shore in Bohemia, here: GHAZEEPORE RD.

# The mahogany ship
*in memory of John Manifold*

How I would have the poem rest:
that European circumstance, the ship
storm-blind
and unaccompanied
beating along by shelved cliffs, gulfs, west
under the gales' whip,
the length of her
urged at the last ashore
prow abutted on hummocks
of sift, to burrow like a burr.

And the passionate connection to begin:
thrown once for all too far up to be manned,
sea-jarrings
and the speaking charts
of sea-roads stilled, their known ports shunned to earn
a pilgrimage in sand –
the timbers weigh,
sailors run crouching, bayed
by fears, and snatch at brush
for watch-fires in her lee –

night-long at the flickering edge
of their race and language. Fires sicken. The dark
land dawns,
dunes packed by rain
mass, shoulder aside Europe. At the ridge
a face flares, turning last
from sand-bloated breakers
after water, timber, game.
Un-history cancels them. The Yangery
like the long wind hurling and raking

take them, unravel and stow
their genes between the dark thighs of the tribe.
Coast songs
and the wry cross
possess their children, the songless ship-ropes go
for nets that childbearing wives
three centuries on
re-knot for fishing – Jim Cain's
black Kitty and yellow Nellie – in their flesh.
Captain Mills notes the strain

surfacing, a legend's landfall,
even while the wind-grey panels of the hull
knives slip on
and farmers pillage
wear out of sight like the Great Expedition, founder
in wastes, and bearings fail.
The poem, consigned
and claimed, deepening in sand,
shifting, reaches among layers
to a beginning, to ends . . .

The long stain in the mind.

---

This wreck, observed many times between 1830 and 1890, lay among coastal sand-dunes near Warrnambool. It was in the tribal land of the Yangery, among whom Europeans thought they saw Caucasian alongside Aboriginal physical characteristics. The ship's remains have disappeared, though good bearings were taken on it and several expeditions have tried to locate it.

The Portuguese Grand Expedition of 1536, led by Cristobal de Medonça, is a possible origin of the wreck. The voyage, coasting eastern Australia, was in "illegal" longitudes (on the Spanish half of the globe) and therefore secret. K.G. McIntyre's *The Secret Discovery of Australia* (Picador) and J.K. Loney's pamphlet *The Mahogany Ship* (Marine History Publications) are my sources.

# The White Room

1982–1986

*I start to print*

# The white room

Speaking softly speaking
softly in the white room in your ear
through the window where sunlit curtains blow
out to the full fields that will lie dank and darken under snow

I am speaking softly to you here
curling into the process of your mind
feeling to where it links it moves over will never be undone
never will your hearing being be again as it was here
    now I have come in

# Practising incapacity

Hand raised
to the switch, as the lamp clicked off —
she stood amazed

at light still hived in the shade
and rayed on the wall;
then it had faded —
it was nothing, nothing at all

but what nerve-slowness and incapacity made,
the retina's after-image. So she played
at making the light stay,
at looking hard,
and every time the bright floss melted
faster for being pursued.

Like the miraculous and skimming flight
of the dreaming will —
though it is said it is a sexual
figuring, dreamers cannot
measure what need or weather is its fuel;
yet they invoke it night by night.

# The night rumour

There it is again, an upward draught, faint as light breathed against the night clouds, particular as the spark lacquered on every fleck of rain let fall, let fall, let fall through the shifting probe of headlamps or before the unwinking red lights.

The night rumour courses wide, exhaled from the suburbs of attention. Here they drive communing in the car's penumbra, ghostly above the dash; there over coffee they confide a scruple about the last scene. The rumour goes about.

It is later, it is really late. The foyers are darkened, their leadlights a scribble on fish-grey, raked by a stipple of gleams from outside — a tram to the depot?

Muted now. The summer insects, scratching of vines on boards, running-noises of refrigerators and street-lamps, the turning of sleepers. The poorest performer at life is an acrobat, as the rumour slung across moonless gardens and beneath roofs sets swinging the old longings, notions let slip, tomorrows unfounded. And nothing — screened, doused, forgone, forgotten — need be hidden now. Neither the cockroach eaten by ants under a corner of the lino nor the schoolgirl you wanted to be best friends with, years ago, and stole her pink pencil eraser instead.

Miniscule, endlessly re-connecting and changing impulses within the city's slowed being, they are yours in the unlit room. It is this the city-bred yearn for and come back to. This life you wrap round your own.

# Night talk

With midnight voice I lean after children: Where
shouldering what dark and by what sign
are you walking? Is it the hill track?
Which way have you turned your face?

Voices cross, young, voices of parents, no
thread nor threat of handhold left,
unquiet, calling Who shall be now
my wakening and my rest?

The children laugh, alight with their beacon sex,
away in the din and shine of their energies.
Our voices mesh like rain, they roam
the sleep of sleepers and the high windows.
Birdcall and morning, we all come down
at a rouse. But the children have gone.

## Crow notes

Ground forager, crow
opens its beak.
Out pops a brief
rusty hinge —
toneless, efficient.
Snaps shut.

Light goes. Crows call
by the greying lake.
They have taken to the trees
their cries, mournful
as thwarted souls,
full-fed.

# A way with birds

Birds came to me;
I gave them names.
Friending! say, Mothering! Teaching!
Sweet callers.

Look how I've pulled out
their long blue tail-feathers.

They strut and pick
just where they used to
because they used to,
guileless unweighted rumps

twitching a little, hatching
long blue tail-feathers.

*Friending. Mothering. Teaching.*

# Passing the island

The man has gone into the island.
The man in the island
has taken a cracked cup
behind the mangroves.

The gold-rimmed cup will learn
to forget tea-sets,
as the mangroves drop seeds
along the mudflats.

On the ferry that never calls
they know his name.
The cup lies on its side
for sun to scour.

# The rat-king

Just another picture that keeps you looking
   intent, properly ill-at-ease
at the seven rats with their tails knotted
   together, a brilliant X-ray,
the bone-threaded spokes of their wheel of life.

Such endings! The still centre of course
   just another puzzle, like
the bog-people's settled tanned features;
   their deaths sorted out
by something in the mind's set, acknowledging

stored peat-bogs — bog-tribute, bog-ritual —
   and the frantic rat-huddle
a solution taken too icy seriously
   before the frantic centrifuge
slowed under winter's precept: play it cool.

## At home, beloved

She walks the house in her mind *disaster*
she tries the doors mutters *horror*
she shouts *murder*
*murder* she howls *murder murder wreck*
*ruin ruined nothing no* she calls
and to whom *no no no why*
the sun lays silence on the floors
the sun muffles the drip-stained glass
the sun with its silly grin in the garden
*the end* rocking *the end ruin no*
*where* nobody can tell her
she couldn't tell them either
a very polite cheery woman
full of energy full of ideas.

# The bird of night

calls like a mocking son
but goes on too long.

I eat the meal of resentment,
I am the cache of discontent –

do not bury me under the cornerstone.
Do not plump me on sofas. Do not salt me.

I am ill to lie with, I turn
in the gut, I sour in the good season.

The lines show, the talents run
irremediable as grass-stains,

smears of tomato and blackcurrant.
The birds of day ping and scratch.

# The end of the lift

Beyond the trees — the drop.

There was the cold oldie with white sores
called superannuation. And his mate,
sympathetic boy lit up on distance, she noted.
The respectable familiar dressed to disarm
talked his way to a footing, then shoved at her ribs.
Not for real. Joke of course. When they left the car
she walked. They didn't need to drag or prod.
She walked right on without a stop. She'd known
them all quite well, this payoff. After the ridge
of tortuous pines, a space, the balding height —
how far? Among the trunks crouched, further on,
tumour-face, fire-paced in a charring humour,
easy as spilled oil, roadside wait-and-see. She
face up took the one path, documented
a while by their seedy sleeves, for once not talking,
looking up, boughs spars sticks, smaller and more
dark, a startled cloud . . .

# Getting back from the outing

Not the outing, however
festooned with koalas, photos
and sunlight, stayed with me waking
but the getting back. You went off
and my walk to the main road
fetched the pursuer, giant
show-car chrome-barred on scarlet
that came at me battering, then backing
and battering again at my alcove
where it opened behind me, dream brick,
never a dint from the battering . . .
danger! the invisible driver
knew his name and drew off,
me pursuing now, somehow
here we are, dead-end, a small room,
the car is a little boy,
I'm waving, how could I, this golf-club
of leather, it creaks wth stitching,
it bends with its unthorough stuffing
and I who started for home –
lamenting, swiping, lamenting,
left facing the child: Why can't I
hit you? why can't I hit you?

# Day with one cloud

The size of a man's hand.
This little spade, bright red,
bought as they went to bathe
and broken at the spathe
has become what she said,
the stepmother on the sand

(and no-one thought it funny)
over her toddler's play
to the seven-year-old not hers:
You will replace it, of course,
as he gasped at the break,
with your own money.

Exact in her dealings
she accounted for the day
though his Dad has a hand for each.
She took up the shards from the beach.
She has never touched the boy
unless told to. As for feelings –

eyed from above,
graceless, dumb with dismay,
he needs. He can't yet see
her recoil as kin. They agree
on the babe's intelligence and grace,
the child of love.

# In-flight note

*Kitten*, writes the mousy boy in his neat
fawn casuals sitting beside me on the flight,
neatly, *I can't give up everything just like that.*
Everything, how much was it? and just like what?
Did she cool it or walk out? loosen her hand from his tight
white-knuckled hand, or not meet him, just as he thought
*You mean far too much to me. I can't forget
the four months we've known each other*. No, he won't eat,
finally he pays — pale, careful, distraught —
for a beer, turns over the pad on the page he wrote
and sleeps a bit. Or dreams of his Sydney cat.
The pad cost one dollar twenty. He wakes to write
*It's naive to think we could be just good friends.*
Pages and pages. And so the whole world ends.

# All that carolling about the Christ child


The dream was about grown children, lots, and the doctor
come at mid-morning (primeval home-visits, in dreams
you don't quibble about bills) to do check-ups.
   And the baby dancing in my arms.

I'd left the flight to Egypt for him to fix up.
Everyone beamed, and what about a name?
The doctor in her drab coat and half-smile
  made the stethoscope small enough,

neatly but why? and offered no suggestions.
The baby trod my fingers, groped for my hair,
threading me: by this you are sewn in the signature
and to the last stitch; by this you are saved.
   All questions settled by angel
   and no need of crucifixions.

# Mentors
*for Andrew Donald*

Are they from god? Are they lonely? These yelps let slip
will savage me yet. You ask me to explain mentors.

There's their habit of walking round the corner, mid-
  phrase, scenting
encounters, pronouncements you can finish yourself.

How they're seen ahead and moving, fleshed with purpose;
the shadow growing, even when the mover's still.

Prepare to keep interviewing to fill the place.
Tireless mentors are awarded a cross, or hemlock.

From gods or God? Refer to the mentor in question,
or to writers of text-books, rarely in the same building.

Store – rest sent – stone – stem – torn son – tensor –
torment – storm – I tremble at mentors' omens.

To stand: you stand in the circle of your mentors.
To walk: they leave. You have light. You walk alone.

# Answer to Why?
*for Rebeca*

It's all too hard,
said God,
and pointed at the devil.
The test is at his level,
why don't you ask him?

Of course I never
gave my personal fiat
that you had to be fat
or thin.
Are you sure you are?
What — love?
and food? Isn't it good enough?
Oh, food for the world.
It's a vicious circle
that,
it's state of the art,
it's great technology,
it's all in the too-hard basket,
it's the agencies.

Have you personally,
asked God,
got a BOMB?


I mean,
it's obviously
someone else's fault.
Long-term predictions?
I don't like to scold, but
TAKE IT TO THE DEPARTMENT
OF HEAVENLY FICTIONS!

Next please . . .

# The journey with children
*for Sibila and Richard*

You have tickets this time for the children. You mean
    to be known
by them in the seasons and cities of your race —
Europe, that further memory; you draw them a face
of roads, with place-names; ritual, passing on.

Experience nests in the branches of expectation.
You do not expect the places to be the same,
even the museums. And they are not the same.
What has been added is the children. At last your decisions

are upon you: time to remark only the best,
or what calls you again with the true remembered voice.
But your ear is no longer in question. The question and choice
are the children's. Your talk of the journey will be obsessed

with their fascinations. You scarcely can guess their reasons
but you guess. Their eyes are your new museum of taste,
young leaf in ancient gardens. You lean to be embraced
and grow there unnoted in their flowering season.

# The letter from America

The letter from America
drops in the box.
The family is impressed.
The postie walks on
uplifted by the revelatory postmark
and stamps from America.

Someone in the house
stands unlit watching
for just these wings
and a personal print-out
of the state of nations, affections
and rates of exchange.

The letter is orbiting stars
here and America.
Our sightings are less frequent.
When it nears
conditions are unstable,
the static abhorrent.

The letter from America
has made an incision
along the threshold.
It applies reassuring
suggestions and alternative promises.
It encloses a contract.

No-one will violate
its supersensitive triangle.
Suddenly it exploded!
It was so white!
The letter from America has vanished
leaving a zip-code —

someone in the house
is counting the promises,
is hoarding the answer.
Someone in the window
is watching the windy day,
is mourning, is mourning.

# The late lemon tree

All summer the lemon delayed.
Its four bold branches,
parted at knee-height, flourished
large yellowy leaves
just as when bought. Watering
hardly helped, or digging;
a few leaves blundered down,

then flowers, waxen and splayed
showed the flag, meaning nothing –
neither fruit nor forking
of twigs nor tiny bunches
of new leaf. And suddenly now
it's mad autumn, unpinning
everything. That world of green.

# Face for casting
*in memory of Emily Hope*

The twist of candlewax
I worried into a face,
she took and translated —

the long-nosed block
on the north-European model
both our families bred from

she passed her hand over,
and as if the stuff had known
her mind's late mould

(the Nepalese silver-smith's
floor, his images
fetched from web-thin tracings)

the face budded,
lotus and enigma, the blush
of wit and the wakened god

on wax dark from the wick —
a temple-dancer's cheek and lip.
Now that Emily's dead, a hint

for Emily's real look.

# The address
*for Jim Legasse*

Looking him up in the Directory –
the friend, soon to die –

here's name, address, number
on scrap paper. The Address Book's for lasting longer.

She bites her lip. Has slipped from commonest health
forgetting the commonalty of death.

Not, not to serve as true
what's fed through mere today's peep-hole, plainly in view,

frowning, she finds the surname's alphabetical place
for the fickle, still-listed number, the failing address

and futile initials grappled to this man's meaning.
Full stop. This set down, set out; his sacred being.

# Potato-field at Ampton

The potato-plants move at dawn
all the leaf sidling
easy a-glint in the long
fabric of a field.

Tree-rows walk shadowy
short of first furrows
round the vast opening to sun
down eastward

and the near yellow-shooting weed
heavy, taller than those
woods, and the seeding grass
never still

take my deepening eye
less than the stir
of its early moth-flowers and all
the curling interlaced

potato-field, its love a large summer's
cover and clasp
of turned earth and the growing along
spuds underground —

thumb-joints of white winking
if you grub shallow —
but deep, safe from deer-foot
and tread of tractor,

the big ones hatch, crop
slurping the giant
water-plume wheeled out to serve
them.

It ticks round a half-circle,
they
are silent and grin with eyes
farmers' grins,

beside under the near pines
on needles run
a farm of short-tailed pheasants
fattening for autumn,

whose low cheap and ruffling
head-cocking and dithery
coursing's confusedly
mortal — but small

to the offered-up half-mile-long
internodding back-and-forth-brushing
wind-knowing weather-having
earth-and-sky-proving moving

Suffolk potato-field —
to me at dawn opening the door
on grass, some last poppies and lifting birds
it is loving.

# To the city visitors
*for Robyn Archer and Diana Simmonds*

To the city visitors
sights in a field bring starts
of things as they are not –

the bakery furnace air over wheat
a premise of its true nature
headed for bread,

the unsteady spread of the daisied
meadow beyond, a veiled distancing
of those grounds of the big house,
quite supporting theories of class.

Other things we see with reverent
or appalled eye,

the man bent, pouring for the pheasants
something he has brought early in his 4-wheel drive,
and will not be seen again all day,

unassuageable summer reared
in the great oak, our shade here,
winding its dead arms all the more about
than the living, that thicken hid,
and bearing its moss up –
up! (the land's watery habit) in July
after weeks of swallows scissoring clear sky.

Then there's the flint cottage and sheds,
thatch greying to rot,
in a grassy spot between a field and a field
with two oaks, some thorns,
and old roses, jessamine etcetera
masking cobwebbed burrows by the wall
where the death-trap glass

breaks and lets in the desperate doomed swallow
to beat there in a window till it fall
that were every pane gone
looping easy as vine
and touching no wing to frame
would pass . . .

Then there's the fallow deer seen at dusk
just in the standing green crop,
we say came out for us;

and the pheasants we call stupid
making the best
in their wired enclosure under the pines
of every grain;
when they crossed, fluttery and jittered,
KAMIKAZE PHEASANTS we jeered
and leaned to check the striped chicks'
refuge in dry grass
(but we have heard even in our summer
walks among raspberry bushes, the shots).

These things, and their intentions,
we cannot read.

Then there's the turnaround triangle
where the fields meet at the wood.
We stare at the ruts'
odd flints.
They lie unread,
they wait for the event
inscrutably
as cross-roads at Larissa.

# Five poems on memory

Here you come, memory,
with your big bag.
Or is it me staggering
hauling the monster treasure?
Or me there inside?
(Just inside my boundaries
waits last year's woman,
behind my nose, her nose,
further inside, the schoolgirl
with her stained finger callus,
holding the baby, the oldest me, in the dark
like a wooden babushka.)

In a flash
St Elmo's fire, the portent,
touches the taut rigging,
strikes, streaks, leaps,
terrifies the sailors.

I wake up struggling with memory.
Tar and feathers, tar and feathers
stifle and stink and thicken
all over this *nincompoop*
schoolgirl shamed in class
over and over
all over again.

Sunlight is timing my days
but behind me the other light
shadows me, shows me
a dark manikin ahead.
I hurry with arms outstretched
to hold her hurrying
with arms outstretched
past the horizon.

Memory, my good dog, you eat up
the food I have set.
Then we go for a walk.
I have a path in mind;
you have your concerns.
Each course you set
by landmarks I can't discern
hauls at the walk we design
together.

# Bagged giraffe

The giraffe is biting its toe-nails.
Its spots are rubbing off.
Its little horns are caught in the zip!
It mourns,
I will never unfold to graze trees!
It worries,
I'm pregnant, where will I put the twins?
It says,
This may be the smart way to travel
but if you'd cut holes for my legs
I could show you something!
It says,
Nylon foliage is for the birds
or a stomach that's not been invented
so de-invent me, please, at once!

# An old bag, printed "Cynthia"
*for friends at W.A.I.T.*

Look! a cowed shape. Did it hit the ground with guile?
Or chance-wise, simply drop in from on high?
Is it waiting for a hand – and who'll oblige?
It's labelled. No remarks of substance, kind,
or quality. Quantity – medium-size
to us: a small-scale huddled human, say. Min-
ute it's not. Cynthia's it was – but why
did she bring it here, dump it and leave it lying
crumpled, gape downward, for us passers-by
to give a wide berth, purloin, or sanitise
into a bag officialdom's provided
slung in its cylinder, the decade's bright
official colour – roadline yellow? Fine
if suddenly the one, the thing inside
went out of style, smelled bad, or started dying.
You wouldn't want to stop her in full flight
or blame her, finding what the bride of time
unfolds from wedding-skirts, for all the trying –
unfolds, hurts from and hides, time after time.

# The emperor

The Emperor Franz Josef of Austria is clapping
his hands, quietly in the half-light, for a girl to bring
whipped cream for his chocolate, low in the cup.
The hunters are dressing for dinner and the summer-house
　　is bare.
I cannot explain how he got here. He has finished
clapping, and the girl has not come, with her starched ribbons
a sort of Franz-Josef moustache at the small of her back
and her neatest shoes of Heinzi's polishing. Heinzi
is at the bottom of all this, the stable-boys tune in
to the people's wireless, mutterings of Montenegro.
But the girl may well be back, tearful and loyal
to private fortunes, and never know who huddles
spoiled in a fallow grave, grazed over, waste
blood eating seams or seeping unlikely red.

# Floridian Poems

1986

*Growth of seeing*

# Wild shiners

On the road at Narcoossee there's a shop with a pump
and they'll sell me Wild Shiners.

Wild Shiners, says the board out front to me not stopping.
Fish? Fruit?

The college folk can't tell me,
but heaven and earth are following up the notion

suggesting lakes,
Virginia, Osceola, Mizell, Berry, Sylvan, Knowles.

Technology offers the spotlit space-shuttle,
nightly readied, not wild enough,

in the year of the comet, which at least works.
But what will they sell me back at Narcoossee?

Marbles? Gold nuggets? Mad shoe-shine boys?
Or a parish of just husbands

fresh from righteously blackening as many wives' eyes
and ripe to go further?

No, my Wild Shiners
must be sweet as striped humbugs, fine as a fish-lure,

sudden as the hawk
seen in the long field and not seen again.

One morning, when stars are fading at Narcoossee
and Columbia's congressman sleeps in orbit,

some farmer of words will drop by for his board —
his potatoes over, waiting on frosts.

# Zouave marching team, Rollins College, 1913–1914

"Quick and spirited drill" they repeat, no doubt,
weekly on campus. And try their costumes out,
wrong in detail, but always look to the spirit.
War is turning this way — prepare, prepare it!
They have looked for their rig to the Civil War
and the young, would-be grandfathers it did for.

Look at the shy, lit faces having fun;
only *this* might pass as the least bit Algerian.
Busty for jackets, put off by puttees,
Injun headbands for caps, a gipsy wheeze
the cross-tied pumps, and of course skirts,
quite short. Like the recollection that war hurts.

In Perth, the Boer Wars past, my aunt was twelve,
in Assembly with teachers and scores of boys who fell —
the State's best these, the first scholarship school.
Husbands never to wed. And War was announced, and the girls
leapt to their feet and gloriously sang
"Rule Britannia" — this was before Anzac.

# TV sacrament

What is mere life to the media if, full of NASA hype,
starry-eyed teachers, each with spouse and children,
queue up to teach the nations
space is a U.S. playroom?
And the consultant panellists shall accept them.

We stop and stare,
the vibrant group photos are ready for the front page.
The phrases to inspire classrooms have been selected.

We have all the time in the world to memorialise them;
they had no time;
and little enough had
the seven widowed, eleven orphans.

The TV screens are like the nation's stomachs,
ingesting, excreting;
they are not sickened,
they are not foiled of their product,
they have no lack of persons –

the wild space-spider, the explosion,
the bereaved in their enforced decorum,
the experts shoring up careers,
the grief-gurus -

these are the presidential capital,
these are the national family,
the substitutes,
the data,
the lesson.

Gorge, gorge.

# The day the world turned over

It's a party in Florida
not one where big things were planned
and you're not even drinking

A group coming in the door
huddles there
over a photograph
and the exclamations:

Double Bay! Lovely Double Bay!
My Double Bay . . .
I'll be back, not next year, but . . .

And as they free themselves from the glue
that surrounds every photograph,

You remember *that* restaurant!
(and you don't — not that one)

And what's happened?
The world has turned over.
All those years of the Waldorf Astoria,
years of Greenwich Village, Soho,
and not confessing
to kangaroo valley addresses,
the years of acquaintance with pastrami
and knowing where there was good coffee, cheap,
somewhere off Oxford Street —
and then making off
to Oaxaca, Damascus
and the little church at Wells
with the quite extraordinary Jesse-tree.
The world has turned over,

it's your surf-board they're riding
sunburnt and living it up
on authentic Sydney sunlight,

it's your city, your eating-out, your nightspot,
you have no news for them,
the southern secret is out

and you, the exotic, exploded –
they've seen thousands like you,
talked with several
and understood 45 per cent –
so, no revelations!

just a working relationship
and another tourist trap
you're not sure you approve
of their being so damn comfortable in,
now you understand the suffering
of tourist destinations,

and welcome and do come in
and the underhand hope
they won't poke round the roots
or work hard at explanations
and tell you about yourself
or move the d'oyleys . . .
they can suggest changes in the transport
go gaga about aboriginal art
and the opera house
"love the drawl" and stalk emus,
but here's hoping they continue to stick out
like zinc ointment at Manly
and don't ever realise
they don't really understand
and here's hoping
they don't, in the end, like it *that* much.

# A meeting in Winter Park

Mrs Louise Peeler
met among live-oaks along Essex

beside discreet passing of cars
confirmed the call of the cardinal
(red, a bit tousled, up there)

threading it a long shiny bead
several times sweetly
then CHOP chop-CHOP chop-chop-chop-chop-CHOP
and sometimes between beads
a trip a clearing of the throat

I said I was Australian (am)
Yes she said I thought your accent
sounded Australian

met again on Lakeview the sails
she'd taken a layer off
I stripped off my jumper
she on her daily mile
from the Condominium at Mead Gardens
agrees there are birds (starlings)
not welcome at a trough
they couldn't keep up the house
summers in North Carolina
but she being a chilly person
and thinks my landlord's house
beautifully renovated
the varnish not quite in keeping

and now 52 years married
her husband introduced her
to their reading group as a friend:
Mrs Louise Peeler.

# Re-routed in the States

All over the U.S.A.
citizen armies are withdrawing,
narrowed to a stream of wheels –
rout 20, rout 50, I've driven them,
no doubt defeated, making
myself scarce, nudging speed-limits,
and never able to work out why
routs go headlong both ways.

And when John and Jane Doe in Australia
take to their tour-bus or hire-car,
what do they think of the root
their Sydney-side agent scalped them over?
A bit fundamental, roots?
Not in front of the kids, a bit biological?
Though since the man went to Africa and wrote Roots
there's more to it. *And* high-cultural French.

Not a big deal, language, but complicated
if what happens to a defeated army
is, in the U.S., a root.
The joke falls flat, much like
the ignominiously rooted infantryman
skulking behind palmetto on rout 50
and falling over the live-oak root.
Rout. Route. Root.

An army after 49 roots may be discounted;
an army after 49 routs should be disbanded.
It all calls for root-beer, and meditations
in which neither word occurs.

# Bear dream

I slept and dreamed worms big as logs
that turned on men and tossed the dogs;

I slept again and dreamed of bears
that shone and wriggled in their lairs

and dug them down into the mould
and followed rain up to the world

of worms like bears and fish like clouds.
I hear you mutter "Why not birds?"

And oh, the bears at nesting-time,
hemming the nests and chirping rhyme!

# Condominium Poems

*Adult mobile homes*

All flights terminate
in Florida, home of
adult mobile homes.
Everywhere hapless
non-Floridian
States of the Nation
wallow in downpour,
huddle from windchill,
whimper for summer
and call for a weather-caller
calling for sunshine –
tiny mobile thoughts.

All over the Union
you hear them stirring,
dreams of retirement.
Edging off slabs,
hauling at water-pipes
gulping detergent,
jiggling electricals,
exercising the spare bed
heels-up into
the tin-foil bulkhead,
they are not perfect yet –
infant mobile homes.

All along the slipstream
of the Canada geese
you find them in training:
it's mobilisation.
They have grown wheels,
they shuffle away chocks,
they gird on their tow-gear!
They bend their vent-pipes

for avenues and bridges,
they graze along sidewalks
to southern comfort,
dreaming mobile homes.

All national routes
descend into Florida
swollen with legend:
the southern mansion
seen floating south,
steeplechase in the wake
of a nameless hurricane.
The belles and the dudes
live it up on mint juleps
at the top of the staircase
moored somewhere near Cuba
with access to bankers.

At all State borders
they shuck off the children
and start for the beaches.
Here they come, loaded
on Greyhound, on Amtrak,
on Eastern, on Delta!
Here they are, bulging
with worry and luncheons
but planning the salads
wth vitamin-supplements
and drinks at the golf-course!
Adult mobile homes.

All through Florida
the homes are rejoicing
and relaxing from tax-loads.
They will abandon
the mountain summers.
The tow-gear's rusted.
Three plastic gnomes

they're leaving to Homeworld,
their bones will bolster
the Floridian sandbank,
and Otherworld shall raise them up:
adult condominiums.


*No more worries*

Always the bother, going somewhere.
The hassles, to make it a home.
Taking it with us –
the bears for the pillow,
the mutt, the vase, the palm.

Always the trouble furnishing.
The hoops to jump through.
The measurements, the matching,
the regulations, the delivery-schedule.
Relax, relax, we've got a lot of living to do.

Let's short-cut the whole process.
It's a new life, let's go!
And money can do anything
at this end-of-the rainbow
condo!


A limo from the airport
a man on the door
life-memberships for our sport
air-conditioning cooling heating humidifier
    in the ceiling or the floor
and the experts have done the decor!
She doesn't have to worry any more.

Once she's opened the door
I'll never have to give her any more
   always-ever-after gifts
   ever any more!

There's the forks / the knives and place-mats
sheets and cases / in the drawers
a list of flowers / for the table
there's shell-patterns / in the paper
all over / the wall,
the refrigerator's / full —
she'll never have to worry any more!

The man will park / in the basement for us
the dogs at the track / will do the racing for us
the stars are on TV / living romance for us
the day-trips with the agency /
                       have wondrous moments for us
the golf-pro's out there / setting records for us
somewhere / they're growing veg'bles for us
people who can't afford this place / will sin for us
the doorman's rac- / ing tips will win for us
the upstairs laundromat / will wash for us
Neighbourhood Watch / will watch for us.

With their magnificent cerebral-cortical IQ
the dolphins at Marineland
will sing for us, we'll understand
they understand,
(we'll have no)
hoops to jump through,
(we'll pay, she'll see)
in twos and threes
they'll loop the loop for us
(we'll buy the video)
they'll jump through hoops for us
(we'll run the replay)
the hoops to jump through!

We don't have to do a thing any more.
She'll never have to worry, fuss and worry any more,
at the end-of-the-rainbow condo for two!
But what shall we do?

## Viewing at the condominium

The 40-year-old corporation lawyer
is visiting his Mama between trips.
The daughters have visited,
demanding almond in their burecas.
Tonight over whisky and dry
all the old mothers are watching
Miss Teenage U.S.A.!
Tonight on their sofas they are sailing
through lights, back-sets, lights,
a sunburst like a watermelon party!
A fortune in prizes is waiting
for the lucky winner.
The young girls are all friends.
The young girls are all dieted.
They told one another the secrets
of their exercise programmes!
They helped one another
with their colour rinses!
The young girls are not just bodies.
Each of them is making a speech:
   I had this funny mother.
   She was a feminist!
   She had this KINK about beauty contests!
   And I said *MOM*!
   and now my MOM is my biggest fan!
The old mothers are watchng
from the sofas of the condominium.
The lawyer is flying back
to the blue and white china in his east-side condo.

## *The Bolivian lady*

Number Five's a Bolivian lady
who bought in right at the start,
she's not seen her patio lately —
she's off in Paree or La Paz.

The condominium neighbours
are longing to have her reside,
they clear out the mess in the mailbox
and peer at the silence inside,

security has them all worried,
they watch for the consular car —
she's staked it in Buda and Brussels,
Bermuda, Beirut, Bogotá.

Their sisters and friends want the condo,
but for all their dismay and distress
Bolivian ladies will wander
from a safe residential address!

Hurry back, Bolivian lady,
on your llama or cama or jet!
The drapes that you ordered are fading,
the S-bend was never flushed yet,

black widows will mourn in your garage,
your Balenciaga will rot
whether you stay home or travel
and rhumba and samba or not.

The bridge-tables fray in Miami,
the tax-man keeps sending accounts,
the walls of your condo are clammy,
the hurricane's ready to pounce,

the ashes of neighbours fly northwards,
dear lady, the beach-sands are gone,
the Bolivian sucre is falling,
your investment is calling — return!

# Dream houses
*(C'a d'Zan, the Ringling residence at Sarasota, Florida)*

They are always by water, and far from town.
There the marvellous happiness rests on the terrace
like sunlight, and sets each feathered breeze on wing
for a different part of the gardens; and the Gulf
stirs and bears up the boats and the dense islands
on the skyline, the estate's furthest enchanted rim.

At first, they are delightful secrets; at last, they are shown.
We imagine the couple, discovering the lucent anchorage,
breathless with good fortune; here, they agree.
Somehow, the minute there was a really good road
and the invitations were sent for a select house-party
the secret was blown; it was just another place to see,

though of course, happiness smoothed the spiky grass
as we turned at the turreted gates, up the palm-lined avenue.
A trance of happiness, peasant figures in the hedge
by the rose-garden, Venice in the facade.
Marvellous happiness was on the menu
and dancers were painted on the panels overhead

in the corner room, and the lisping waves of the Gulf
glistened and sparkled on at the antique glazing.
Indisputably, marvellous happiness
sharing the circus collection, the old masters
chosen with flair, roasts from huge refrigerators.
Everything there was special; there was always more space,

years for new plans, new talents, breathless guests,
canvases, marble figures, coups at auction;
no oracle then foretold our gossiping guide
on first-name terms with all that stride and wealth.
(John's appetite was huge; the man was common.
And Mabel's taste.) And then the lady died,

and he lived on and saw his fortunes melt,
all but the pictures and the house. Childless,
he left it to the State. A civic dream,
noble or grateful or simply desperate,
the ceramic bird-cage chipped, developers biding
their time, the Twenties sunk, the memories fleeing –

the ringmaster of finance spotlit, the last act,
still hoping to fill a gap in the collection
rolling out masked, the auction catalogues
peopling his night like souls for hairsbreadth judgment,
and a Grand Parade to the measure and the mettle
of unlikely happiness, houses, art, and the odds.

# Poems 1960–1972

including poems from *FOUR POETS*
and *NU-PLASTIK FANFARE RED*

*The broken pane*

# The bush-fiddle

The bush-fiddle's broken.
A thin pale nylon
note unspoken
curls to silence.

The string unswinging
that fished for death
lives transfixed, singing
its onedrawn breath.

Like a sprouting twig
of the mantleshelf
it hangs by a peg
and sings itself.

Tentatively
the little gourd
dreams its symphony
("The Unheard").

Keats would have liked it.
Keats died young.
But it's not unlikely
he knows the tune.

Calmly it ponders
the cold square hearth
and grows to the roundness
of sky and earth.

Its bush-fruit belly
is fat as the sun
and brown as a gully
and quiet as long.

The calabash made once
a coolamon
for a black bush baby;
for me a song

a slow ripe fall
of fruit and tendril
so full so still
I cannot mend it.

# The intellectual traveller

I

So this is where you live. A difficult land
barren yet burgeoning, its ivory hillsides
enamelled with flat buds that have no insides.
The people subtle, swift of thought, but bland;

a world? a paradox. Ascetics walk
the gardens to admire the rococo
flamboyance and its artful libido.
How skilled they are in clean and dirty talk,

how civilised their leisurely defile!
Practical courtyards, elegant facades; astutely
sufficient in nice intangibles of beauty.
Decidedly, the inhabitants live in style.

They fear the waste of natural excess.
Breasts are for suckling; Art and the Others surely
illustrate passion – One observes; which fully
explains a personal distaste for the caress.

Carnality hardly matters; they approve
vicariously when their own lusts importune.
Learning impartiality from fortune
they broadcast hard-won intellectual love,

ungrateful plant, that flowers on tapestries
and fruits on ceilings in admired profusion
then runs to the last seed, echo and allusion:
doomed graft in the barbarous capitals of trees.

II

Why no compulsive image drives
vision towards the man you are
I ask, and answer, actual lives
hardly compel that ruthless glare.

Matt and diffuse the afternoon
webs down a tarnished orangery.
Your gentle Viennese will soon
desert his springtime-bridal tree

for beasts rampant among the flowers
on various grounds, beneath a sun
perverse, oblivious of the hours,
and chandeliers of Paddington

snuffed by the errant equinox.
Sherbet on Athos. Rucksacks, beer.
Observe precariously the box
décolletée for *Rosenkavalier*.

What endless moment shines and shone
always adjacent, all your days?
What one word do you play upon
stammering elaborate paraphrase?

I seem to know you best between
friendships, and nations, trains, and floors,
sunk like a compact stone within
aquariums of swinging doors.

Fluorescence wipes anonymous
whoever enters. Void of face
with modest yet peculiar fuss
he takes the drunkard's unswept place

they carried out an hour ago,
whose storm make blank necessity
of walls, not proper background; so
he had to leave improperly.

Urbanely your compatriot
resumes the conversational tone
native to limbo's halls, though not
cosmopolitan as your own.

His gaze rears enigmatic twins:
yourself, unconscious of disguise.
However quietly you inch
towards that careless equipoise,

however circumspectly try
that innocence, you'll see his traits
raddled with personality
foul with immoderate claims of race;

the usual sentiments confirm
his train. Doors shrug round a vacation.
Tubes flicker; others may discern
fulfilment in a destination.

Preferring always to inspire
inverse beatitudes, you come
to choose the precincts of desire,
exact damnation's waiting-room.

# Horses to the sea: a Romantic motif

Horses to the sea
compel us to beginnings.
Venturing down some blue morning
among rooms of salt-swagged nets
shadowing sand, they come
to the edge of silence;
their riders never turn
but face the glimmer of a threshold,
slim island men
held to their Pacific.

That makes a yielding,
wind-razed brown
shaped upon themes of bone
putting off urgency
for the slow rake and sweep of watery time,
long backward seasons' wider undertow.

By other shores
paired coursers leap apart
recoiling from a past
gloom of oblivious force.
No reeds descend their sands.
Hooves crack at crests,
the Moor's clamped on his choice
whipped with the manes.
Sideways and back they curve and glare until
they tighten upon the screaming-point of will.

The sea is always further, never far,
compelling us to beginnings
alike in Gauguin and in Delacroix.

# For Hazim Abdullah

By what right do we intend
the end of a beginning,
the last stitch of any seam,
even the simplest rhyme?
for the little boy died.

That morning they'd been clapping
and he dancing unsteadily
on the cool floor. Fever
struck him aside for ever;
try to forget his laughter.

Where was the interim –
that now, this afterwards?
Can anything be fulfilled;
is fulfilment anything?
you will never ask him.

The child is dead, and questions
waste us with waiting.
Wisdom grows fat on the nonsense
songs we shall make for feet
unborn and unafraid.

# My grandmother

*My grandmother retraces evolutionary paths*

Ah! says my grandmother to the felled tree,
the wind betrays us both:
your lungs wither, my leaves unvisited,
fruitless the roots' groping,
folly my every bite!
Stiff-jointed cousin, exult,
on this slope we have tumbled together.
Is there humility to abide
the lost foothold plummeting down and back?
no pyre, no spark,
the shapeless mouldering valley's ignominious
hordes of slow coal.

*Her village*

At Silverstone the racing-cars
roar and drone and drone and roar,
mad insects wound up for perpetual spring.
It was not so before the War.

Towcester astride the Roman road
drowses, the cars shift up a note
past market, pastry-cooks and inns and flowers,
police-station and the new estate.

All around Whittlebury has changed.
Bowsers beside the Fox and Hounds,
mean 'forties bungalows, glazed heated houses
frankly beset the seasoned land.

The church draws deeper into quiet
up in its wide graveyard. Ignored
the Lodge stands shut beyond its playing-fields.
The pub serves transients, unadmired;

the cottagers commute; the vicar
visits two parishes; the boys
whose school replaced the family, are gone;
the district nurse's area grows.

Old Mrs Solesbury has shut up shop:
the tinkling knockered door, skew shutters,
limp towers of tins and cartons where she fumbled
bent double, all cleared at last. No matter,

the old man died first, and sales of sweets
lapsed with the school. A mental home
they would have made it, but for the petition;
and now they plan an aerodrome

three miles away. With luck, motels
motorways air-chefs terminal
will scream unheeded round my deaf grandmother;
her place incur her funeral.

## She speaks

Don't you think, my dear, said my grandmother,
that I am very old? So many winters
and gifts of potted plants flowering,
so many dear children coming, from the farm,
from town, from childhoods in Australia,
to speak in my deaf ears, to wear
the faces of my sons. The four so faithful,
we went to church together, such an old woman,
when dear Gerald was here. I used to think
it would be sinful to complain, my dear,
of being old; and then Queen Mary said
it was a perfect nuisance! If she thought
it right to say so, then perhaps I may.
My sight so bad, I cannot even read

books of the dear Queen. But the grandchildren and kind friends often come, I am not dull, such an old woman, yet another spring.

# Aussie returns, 1969

Finding his sweet Dee lying, sunshine girl,
flat as a surf-board, fainter than Fanny Hill
swooned on the marge t'await her half-drowned swain's
resurgence — Aussie returned might well fall on!
These days, no petticoats or kerchiefs prose
the poetry of climax, triumph, repose.

Return's the trouble. Virgin he never was,
but once ignored subtleties in joys of force;
the day was when his Dee, conscious or not,
sufficed him, sober or drunken, one or both.
But now, he waits to hear her clarion voice
uplifted to chiack the wet-jowled boys;

and firstly wonders at its carrying-power,
thin and uncompromising as barbed wire;
next, through her thickets of conventional views
unflinchingly advanced, discerns abuse,
promiscuous lush gullies scorched to waste
heartily unredeemed by heart or taste.

She's a hard case. Her magpie harshness drowns
for her, the dusty silence of her towns,
jerks moribund suburban afternoons
towards pantomimes of living, raises stones
to people credibly the backblocks years.
Her voice must shout down death, and can't do tears.

Her chuckle shocks, her sigh's a windy spasm,
her whining strident, thunderous her confusion.
Only some courtesies learned in the baby-carriage
she'll practise softly, shame-faced, then disparage;
well-drilled, respects the hand that rakes the cup
sideways again, and sprints to "Fill 'er up".

Doubtfully ponders our experienced Aussie:
her ochred grin, what does it mean? Because he
longs to assess the changes in his mind,
he mentions Aborigines, extends
his talk to Affluence, Asia and the Bomb;
she snickers. Wadaya know, ya just a Pom!

Wasstopping ya, y'ole bastard! (Gone all shy,
must be that fog, she thinks.) An earthquake sigh,
his frightened sympathy, her thoughts outlined:
nice landscaped block, "Colonial mansion", chimes
to enter by, patio, bar and barbecue,
own bathrooms, built-in 'robes, cars, swimming-pool,

and Dee, the sun-bronzed hostess, twitching flowers
beneath a Namatjira. Stark soils glower
in both, scoured, unrelieved: a womb, a grave.
(The reproduction lives, dates and will change.)
Sudden recession from unfocussed eyes:
Dee as a tiny corpse, mouthing. Aussie flies.

# Getting home

Walking, to see
live grass trailed into swathes by tractors,
the weed-lipped trench widening, and over there
trees in their right bulk — from low down.
In the bare school-ground yellow bulldozers
lurch, smash, pile, prepare
levels for seeding.
>So I was late for driving home,
>and you drove off!
>Beware what you have repossessed me of.
>It is a home to walk untimed, alone.

Seeing
wire-netting speckled with inconstant sparrows;
cars round the junction, drop behind the rise.
A schoolboy leads out silver handlebars,
leans, leans again, recedes.
>So my one friend is in a huff
>I can make nothing of.
>Retreat ebbs everywhere.
>Seeing you varied is a kind of love.

To go
beside little entrances to lawns, left hand
brushing leaves furred or shiny, walk
people's boundaries, their measures set
against all wanderers and homelessness;
perhaps get to know
what it is, about breaking and binding work
(the only kind that welcomes in the worm)
graces our oldest landscape of content.
Well, I can understand
a fence or so.
>So we are home together
>and can broach things there;
>I see no end to planting and repair
>in our green garden.

# Nu-plastik Fanfare Red

I declare myself:
I am painting my room red.
Because they haven't any
flat red suitable for interiors,
because their acres of colour-card
are snowy with daylight only,
because it will look like Danger! Explosives,
or would you prefer a basement cabaret?
a decent home where Italians moved in,
Como perhaps (yes, I've gilded the mirror)
or simply infernal –

I rejoice to be doing it
with quick-drying plastic,
for small area decoration.
I tear at the wall, brush speeding:
let's expand this limited stuff!
It dries impetuously in patches,
I at edges too late scrub; this is a fight.
I sought the conditions,
and the unbroken wall is yet to come.
Clear stretches screech into clots,
streak into smokiness.
Botched job this, my instant
hell! and no re-sale value, Dad;
cliché too. Well, too bad.

It's satisfying to note
this mix is right for pottery.
Good glad shock of seeing
that red-figure vases *are*.
Not 4th-edition-earthy, but stab-colour,
new-vine, red-Attis-flower, the full howl.
My inward amphora!

Even thus shyly to surface:
up we go red, flag-balloon,
broomstick-rocket!
Brandishing blood and fire, pumping
lungs external as leaves!
This is a red land, sour
with blood it has not shed,
money not lost, risks evaded,
blood it has forgotten, dried
in furnace airs that vainly
figure (since mines are doing well)
the fire. Torpor
of a disallowed abortion.

Why not a red room?

# Drums in the suburb

Saturday afternoons
the boy over the road
going on twelve
drums
in his father's cool
double garage
from lunchtime
till darkness
the sun whirrs on

he's at it hard
sat on the line
of sun and shadow
light going in
to darkness
the skins ring
race defaces
tattoo-mulattoes
the neighbourhood

and him outclassing
squared at its shut door
that affront to darkness
his father's car
is to say
daddy own self's
dumb drum
the other side behind him
running to darkness'

revolt! with
his dandy silver
assault and battery
dim-spun drums
going in for darkness
halt and hum
knock and (oddity) prop
on then and bolting . . .
what goings-on!

his weekend friend
arriving with electronic
guitar hardly
jars the African
under-jungle thump
or Hindu hubbub
as he tunes
to shake up Australian
Saturday afternoons.

# Afternoon suburb, framed by kitchen

I chivvy fat slicks of margarine
over a plughole rim, and eye
splayed death for an eternity
of zooming fly. The afternoon
drags at my sides, wedged here between
jobs and meals,
dusty fly-mesh and spreading workday heels.

Effort spins out the slack gaze, far
across the mound with its rack of tiles,
flicking at scant gums — shreds of fur
formed to their countryside before —
and rasps tight where pines tear
the opaque view
of sky-high greasy circumambient blue.

Those spiring tufts, impassioned still,
close dark and strict — old barricades
that walled a homestead on the hill
and its garden promenade, from wind;
the gold home acre then, the world
now to nuns that built
their cloister congruent with the tree-veined vault.

The suburb bulks, hangs in my flesh,
subdividing, silently trafficked, weighted
with sun. And blood could not beat less,
going by vibrations. It might be this
to hold the strange-featured sly-pulsed
residue of rape,
bear what world's brute imposed — its hope, our shape.

# Black and white, mostly white

How strangely strut
on days of mild lifting air
our white refusals: watts
rammed down an eye's well;
scorings of a traffic-glove index
chastening abandoned ways
kerbed henceforth to bear
only blanched bridals
processionally ambulant . . .

how amazedly haunt
glades of the soul, rumours
of pallid night, and day
swarthy, our colours awry
in frenzies of late neon
and noon's sealed cell.
Agreed rituals shawl
shadow about our houses,
coil light inside.

Houses are not for hiding.
Air coloured clear
passing through intimates
wide green, lofty blue.
But trellis and blind remain
to propose that screened and slit
and safe, we occupy
plastered pigeon-holes, white-
ceilinged, white-silled, unremitting −

you'd need to be limed to the soul
to be there without notice:
neat as eggs, null as ever and ever.
Hiding, for flesh and blood
and mind, means finding
flesh and blood and mind
blood-coloured, to bleed on. Vines
tower above whitewash-shovers.
This poem is not about houses.

# Talking of people

Talking of people I love
I grope for traits
to dignify and endear them, move
you nearer my place
where it's a celebration to forgive.

And I always fail. I'm staggered
when I start cads,
bigots, hypocrites, blackguards
with my unwary words.
Phrasing all of anyone's a hazard;

their music comes so varied
its takes thousands
of listening moods to be married
or related. Vows and
gene-sharing have miscarried

oftener, worse than foetuses.
Though you sometimes purchase
illusion, weeding a field that has
upstanding virtues,
there's a hardy strain in weaknesses

at least for loving: they're funny,
they last. Classic
folly — perhaps too giddy
for most — emphatically
disgracing us graces the randy

centuries that, hot after living,
warm immortal
gossip, and our rage for believing.
May I glow gaudy
in the spate of a friend's forgiving!

# Open-air cinema

As we walked down warm streets
under the splendiferous bougainvillea
    and the rarely-edible ackee
we scanned our multiple bargain, fluorescent
five films, galaxies of stars
in Polypanoramavision and Multistereophonic sound; first,

a Western to get us settled; then
pagans with martyrs, their exotic loves; on to
domestic antics, froth with lashings of scandal
to whip us over midnight; next,
crime-thriller cut for time, but who'd be up to it; and
horror-fantasy, stumpy centipedes
vomiting, their intelligent goggle-eyes
ruined at 3am by the lucky last ray-gun.

Fate of the race, run in seven hours;
then home again
we walk up warm streets
under the reawakening bougainvillea
    and the rarely-edible ackee
to doze through dawn and the barking of small lizards.

# June 1970

In the month of the breaking of mountains, Peru desolate,
and the cracks spilled everywhere outward, nudging
    and lapping
our jarrah thresholds, in the month that confirmed My Lai;
the Pentagon went on recruiting, posting young leaders
set up with machine-guns, missives from gangland Chicago
down a straight street to the villages, to consort with hatreds
that never wink, sidling along by the paddy-fields.
We smelled the swollen dead in the mud-sweeps of Yungay
and the red-holed dead, the mothers and older children
on top of the children that died then; the ones that lived then
spitted in hope and running: delivered extravagantly,
a straight whole clip per child, where it wasn't sharp-shooting.
And we heard the helicopters dip and review them all
and descend for them all, for all of them, all that there were
that had breath to abide conclusions; the months go over
venting and voiding on children the bullet in the clip,
new tremor in the ruin of lake-eyed valleys. Few
will be found to say this month was worse than the others.

# Nothing a child does

Nothing a child does or does not do,
no trick of a child's smiling or a child's speaking
nudges us, glints: this one. In a year or two
he will be nothing. A smudge, a hitch in our breathing

as we glance back, if we dare to, never too long
in case we should catch the movement, incur the acquaintance
of the finally unremitting seducers that wrong
our dreams with dust, our songs with their toneless
    sentence . . .

Nothing in the child forbids, saying Love me less,
invest less, pity yourselves for the space you are clearing
me, to be waste the more for your lovingness.
Nothing begs, Find me more faith to receive the meaning

of the strange man's hand on the bare and silent track
or the bleeding they can't cure yet, than you can hold to.
Teach me to walk shadow-lines, always gazing back
through hangings of shattered web, fouled drops, green heaps
    that moulder,

teach me to be the death I must die to you.
We teach, he learns, whether he takes some hidden
turning-aside we missed, or assumes the due
heaviness of continuing – raptures, guilt

no-one can walk safe from, and nothing invoke
surely and to the instant and degree. And nothing
blurs the fascination of the blasphemous joke
the futureless face of a child fits to our loving.

# Centipede

Sat in my red room with a centipede,
I've no idea when he'll come out;
from the spine of which book,
from the entrails of which chair.
But he's there.

I flapped the slats of a plastic fly-swat
at his multitudinous crescent on the floor.
I had never seen a centipede before.
His fringe of oars surged on in clumps, he veered
and vanished.

Since then I have worn shoes to sit at my desk.
My study attends him, supine and suburban
to his glamour of fangs, his avenue of legs,
the spans of his back and his multiple head in procession.
What has happened

is that till the world's ribs unfasten we closet together,
he and I, eye to eye, prospecting our plaster crevice.
Though I looked up his Latin and habits, not niched in a book
nor tacking a threadbare lap of blue-matted floor
he shines now,

but steers all levels to the abominable fall
that is fear. A finger's length of segments rustling
with centipede intent, stirs in my head;
dark jewel, he has always festered there.
I scan my wall.

# Verandahs

## *Eighties pub*

Grandly, three paces wide
verandahs of country pubs
once skirted their premises, portly
as wives of licensees —
iron-seamed, iron-bugled, iron-
fluted and -fringed, all consequence and bustle.
The whole spread's rusted now, worked loose and buckled
or sagged. But stood.

Years weigh, kids climb, storms club
staid guttering with dead wood.
Each day heaps brittle leaves.
Possums scamper short-cuts
noisy and unconcerned
from pepperina to pipe to eave to roof-tree.
Curt and incurious, glazed in the cafe, tourists
stare out at trucks.

## *Sunflowers in iron*

Myrtle for Horace, he'd learned; for Homer, bays.
They reason, home must be
garlanded with sunflowers
unbending, many-seeding.

The ornate verandah's all accommodation —
waxed (sliding on sacks) for dancers,
lanterns to the young orchard.
And the firm piano, fainter and fainter.

Sun etches day-long darkness in high doorways,
the festooned room inside
airy as vineyards,
samplers and lacework to rights.

With rectitude, a grace and a gradation:
iron flower-borders twine
under iron-embroidered
rayed head-rests for the fine-drawn uprights.

Boys will sleep out there, and lark with visiting cousins,
but it's they will be boarding in
the sleep-out end
and glazing the rest, in time;

last, to have out Gran's knobbed and rigid grove,
her winters of rust and fret
winds canter through.
The arched leaves clang and snap.

## *Dream-watch*

Under late stars, drained moon
and fitful twilight winds
unwalked
the verandah ledge
shudders at stripes of dawn
that ache, opening over fences
peculiar space, new day,
spun light on sleeping bone,
air all round . . .
                      its slab flutters
like a kettle-lid, vaporous longings
strain at its flange, worry its one hinge;
shrugging away the gimcrack guttering,
frills of thin rail and the maundering disarray
of deck-chairs, the verandah on steel
spars continuing outwards
lifts, powered
by intricacies of the suburban dream;
rises, edges heavenward

stairs trailing, cracks agleam,
to join the pitched echelons
of concrete carpets, the kite-gay upward cemeteries
scattering tended pots and mat-bristles . . .
     but sleepers turn
hearing the first pipe roar, the cistern sigh.
Thousands of households hustle.
Teased in a grid of deadlines
visions of dawn-flight
fray like silk. The terraces
wait sunlit, housewives
recovering day's drift
fuss at their moorings and prepare for sleep.

# Sunday outing

This is a day when patients decline to play games.
Not positively windy, nor cold, but the day remembers winter
and the apricot's long new sproutings learn it. Indeterminate
Sunday morning bears on to afternoon,
our plans blot dry and disappear. Hours
so nearly without a mood, we meditate rescues;
these futile outings, sudden and headstrong as suicide.

# Sojourners at Phoenix

They are here, Svetlana, as they were there.
Men, difficult to love. Difficult not to.

Slavers strung out in harness, iron-galled;
smiths of ideals, lining up at the anvil for thrashing.

Stalin, that fathered five-year plans and prisons.
And an architect of together. You can't say fairer.

And when you left, Svetlana, and when you left
with nothing ahead but maybe

glimmer in the jaws of the escape hatch
you could not perhaps slip through whole,

and beyond, the gullet of daylight
convulsed towards brash emanations . . .

and when you left, to be resurrected in person
denying the official schedules for fulfilment,

did not pity and self-pity, pity and self-pity
squelch and pull at your shoe-soles?

And you said, Not again, I will never walk slow there again,
with the sour ideals to sicken of, love to pry loose;

too many people are dead, and some alive,
and I have my daughter.

Another time I will walk wide.
Time fronts up

in your baby daughter's eyes of a head of state,
in their own architecture of partings.

O peremptory daughters of men,
sojourners at Phoenix.

# *Water Life*
## 1972–1975

*Water Life*

# About this woman:

green-eyed and could not give them to her children,
caresses her friends in thought, doubts they do likewise,
malingers and charms in fits and starts, dies daily.

About this woman:
wears no ring. Hangs on her husband, hang him,
to be the husband he could be, if he was;
if it takes fifty years. Faithfully mangles him
in words and thoughts, precarious vindications.

About this woman:
has heard of nymphs like wine; savagely inside
copes with turbid storm-water, and walls of sludge
it piled and can't shift now. The calm nymphs braid
light-runnels, a summer stilled. She dredges
in mixed minds at a quarry-mount of muddle:
where to dump, where gouge, whether
to abandon the site to flood,
worked faces flayed
with rubble in the flurry;

this woman.
Tuned to a tangible mode,
score half-composed, corrupt,
exultant, inharmonious, full of trouble . . .

# Rebeca in a mirror

Our little tantrum, flushed and misery-hollow,
sits having it out
in a mirror; drawn stiff as it
till her joke of a body, from flat,
flaps with the spasms of crying.
The small eyes frighten
the small eyes clutching
out of such puffed intensity of rage.
She will not look at people about, or follow
a dangled toy. No-one can budge her huge
fury of refusal; being accustomed
to orchards of encouraging faces rolled in her lap,
cloud-bursts of ministering teats and spoons
and the pair of deft pin-welding scavengers
that keep her clean,
she is appalled by her own lonely image.
And we, that she's into
this share of knowledge,
and is ridiculously
comic in her self-feeding anger,
her frantic
blindness by now to the refuge
of a dozen anchoring shoulders and outheld hands,
vassals,
her multitudes . . .

Yet who can be more alone, months walled
in her cot's white straw,
the family hushed
and hovering, afraid to touch
so small
a trigger of uproar;
or so much as flutter
one of her million or more

petulant rufflers spoiling for noise and action
around the nerve-end flares that signal ruction?
And think, she has not long come
through a year of twilight time in one gradual place
further and faster
than death, or the endless relays
of causeless disaster;
frail-cauled, a hero, past perils vaster than space
she has come –
and can never re-enter
the unasked bodily friendship
of her first home.

# The scissors
*for Zoë*

Taken with the others, she's the alien;
you adore her, star-faced tyrant, or abhor.
She is paying me out for my dark tutoring of her —
tries scissors on her arm to test our bargain,
looks me in the eye. I see myself
older than her, with nail-scissors, waiting for blood
to dot in fat little holes on my wrist, done alone
for the scar and interest. Like this too, for a dare:
Stop me, God. Try to. (Can you abuse too far?)
She has taken me aback, across, to knowing more
about daughtering, about the connection, prefiguring her
delighted firework. Even when I copy my mother's
cold water way with hysterics, I celebrate Mine
from her foghorn voice to her turn-in fling of the left foot,
from her arch affectionate gusts to her positive blood,
apt hand and greedy eye-play. Brown to my green.

# Polar

As near as dammit to midday
and out of a clear sky;
the casual approach had me in there,
craning to keep with
the tall girl in a pink gingham
skirt sauntering
south to my 50 – 40 – 35
north on Wai-ora,
the easing back exactly sufficient
to keep her covered, all
but a heel, swung hair and the air of smugness
about a telegraph pole;
which is a pretty good reason to dig
poles up and burn them, only
that was all that caught my natural adoration
in a half-hour drive, so
till I hit a pole, following pink gingham
at the corner of my eye,
maybe it's as good a reason as any
for keeping them.

# Charm: to receive a letter

Anxiously owed a letter, balancing
good news and bad — the let-down, the lift,
the jolt, and the stringing-along —
trust it to come
for months

but don't write. Remember, you couldn't care less.
You tot up dates, guess at news, not attending
to the never-of-course-to-be-shaken
message-wagged grapevine;
maintain

the martyr's air, aware of merit but humble.
Ripen reproaches, clutch — dig them under;
write, tear it up. Such fits
churn the grudge thick,
make it stick.

Finally, patience to tatters, past assuming
causes out of varieties of human
breakdown, hiatus, crisis,
whatever — throw pride in
by writing,

straining back rancour. Send. The letter-box
offers straightway the word your opposite
wrote, to the hour, on the spell's end.
(At expense of baring
your caring.)

# Lying late Sunday morning
*for Fabio Rodriguez*

Encapsuled in morning sloth, our daughters gone
at their chancy trot down the passage, to clamber for apples
over toybox and bookshelf, and wind up the world of noise;
propped on our blanketed strand, the brass bed clear
of a junkheap of shoes and overblown gardens of hankies
and socks and a dead-dog stool, we are left to graze
fatness of age and sun.

Look! at the top of our rising field of tiles
taking off east, black as print, there stand at tactics
magpies, you might say, knowing no second word.
Two of them fit to release from a hand, but the big fellow
a lump like a bucket, a beak to terrorize backblocks
decades of Goldilocks gleaming to school, with his lurch
and his sawmill shriek and his spiking

beating down out of windbreak pines. But this raider
has mislaid his joystick. It glints in the anyhow mess
of his nest, forgotten, while he glowers and ruffles and
    hunches,
tail-feathers half-mast. We quell our fears for the quizzical
pair with this goose-heavy lout; then amazed, see one rise,
rocket over, and sputter and stab till the monster launches
sullenly, spitfires at his head.

Well! if that's kindly Nature's morning mood,
give us four whited walls and the floor's disarray.
Or less. Or even more . . . I retreat, I fulfil the enclosure
of your shoulder where I fit, and lie along your side
and from the close order of us see nothing awry,
only how spirited sheets mimic our pleasure
and everything is renewed;

how through the fall and shine of motes, wall
flickers, a little shoal of light-panes swim,
contract to regular chips, then disappear.
On the steady drawer-fronts sun-flecks circle in consort,
their laces of light plucked in time to a mirror's
earth-paced turning; the gilt ray glides on air,
jewels leap in grain, brass flowers; it all

showers from a column of silver facets, a showy
vase of the 1930s rimmed and based
with chrome worn thin by my childhood eye of devotion,
its laundry years, and the puzzled regard of this room
for my stiff-necked indulgence of sentimental taste;
how the dazzles zoom to a course of children's commotion
returning: a Rebeca, a Zoë!

# Flower-poem

After the straight talking-to
after the whining and sulks
after the touch of the rope
after the sneers of defiance
after being lectured and raged at

for sneaky scufflings with his sister
and taunting to tears "little hosts"
and barbarous bumping through the entire
showing of their Daddy's film;
after school-ground dogfights and dudgeon;

he offers, sort of careless,
his by-the-way branch-spoils
committed to a missile of a school-bag
and retrieved now, black-fingered, panting;
two wattle-sprigs, two not;

chooses the goldy mug
and sets it all up, still telling
aloud the leaves' difference,
centres it to a large table-top
and flings off to fresh havoc.

# At the nature-strip

In Lantana Street's mid-morning
an Italian grandmother is trying to happen.

The nature-strip's flat out parching.
All the hardy natives in sight have leaves on;

the garbos were through before the kids went,
the Council street-cleaner's rotary whiskers

slurped by at 6.30. All day begonias
are for nobody, till early each evening hoses them.

Mrs Whatwasitagain in black
is gazing cobbles out of half-melted bitumen,

also whitewash from her hillside village;
and nudging one-language housefronts into gossip

to boast of her Mimo, the smart one,
and of big Vito, tossing pizze downtown,

and Nino, in Bari, who'll be out soon.
Till a carload of shoulders cruising past

bare-faced and noisy as tourists
stalls under her arms-across watching,

worn shoe-heels planted,
head-scarf, and the front-on placid wrinkles;

they pick up in low – leave her standing –
half-focused – an exotic – too old, and simply

out of place. Whose roots settle
for earth, old earth, with a blackboy endurance.

# Occasion for elegy

That was your gibe: I was waiting
for people I knew to die
so as to agonise elegies
and monkey with memory;

but that was when I was younger.
Now I'm near forty, I'm wary
of the body all booby-traps
and the world-wide cemetery,

reminiscence slippery as rot
and loyalty much like libel,
compassion that gobbles down horrors
and suffering worse than I feel.

Most of the dead I can let be.
Rememberers need not raise
and refurbish each part-grimed image
with draperies of phrase.

I grow simpler, I yearn for what's young,
not the death-keyed negative
but light on leaf, and children
that never mean not to live.

# The questioner in black

All the years of her life
she has braved the skull

All the centuries of her civilisation
she has embraced the skull

All the pores of her flesh
she has taunted the skull

Every line of her verse
looks out from the eye-sockets

At the end of the writers' dinner
she rehearses the rising

of black windy song
in the missing throat:

I am still young – nearly,
I write, I am alone,

how shall I live?
how shall I live?

# A lifetime devoted to literature

In your twenties you knew with elegiac certainty
you would die young. Your father's heart attack
tallied, a verification.

Thirty was your worst year: the thirties fatal to genius,
and genius undeclared by the would-be oracles.
You gave thought to publication;

then a news item – friend dropped dead in the street –
coeval, a get-up-and-go editorial
viceroy at thirty-four –

cheered you somehow. You planned aloud and in detail,
publishers ventured for you, reviews came your way
as you learned to joke and your hair thinned,

and several thromboses onward you inhabit unruffled
an active advisory presence: a sitter on Boards
preparing to live for ever.

# In the vanguard

His name I heard rumour'd — the revolutionary poet.
Restor'd to these circles a year now — yet I had not
 encounter'd him —
from the stateside visit. I enquir'd of the host, I view'd him,
trim headband, beard hearty, slab of red-shirted back,
unmodulated robustness; a being declaim'd here;
did his poems come thick-stamp'd, fist-raising manifestoes?
Of his reading I remember how we still'd, leaning forward;
 how the hand —
the hand that had written, his tense and fluttering right
 hand —
gently, constrictedly, from the 3rd to the 4th shirt-button
tripp'd, conducting the inner affectionate harmonies
of a wholly conventional, wistfully sensitive poem.

# Report to the Anthropology Center

Another thing we observed, among the mild
and nervous men and women of this race:
often at the clearing, one would leave a place
in the daily line-up for questioning (hereafter styled
*conference*); and stroll back later on. Quite wild;
our guess is – woodland's made them shy of space.
And many, both women and men, answered with face
null, for no reason – all the while carrying some child
or holding it close. It's possible they gained
security by it, something to hold on to
(probably basically visceral? in their drained
vegetarian way). Where the absentees had gone to,
how the tribal psyche's conditioned on a perch –
these topics need more resources for research.

# How come the truck-loads?

Somehow the tutorial takes an unplanned direction:
anti-Semitism.
A scholastic devil advances the suggestion
that two sides can be found to every question:

Right.
Now, who's an anti-Semite?
One hand.
Late thirties, in the 1960's. Bland.
Let's see now; tell us, on what texts or Jews
do you base your views?
There was a landlord, from Poland, that I had.
Bad?
A shrug. Well, what did he do?
Pretty mean chasing up rent. Ah. Tough.
And who
else? No-one else. One's enough.

# Towards fog

The quality of fog is that it has style but no detail.
Though detected in a state of nuance, it cannot be caught at it.
I try with a 2B – softly – with a 6 or 8B – I am gradual as
 growing –
still there are lines, parts, separations. Fog has none.
When was a photograph of fog, a film of fog moving,
ever so diffuse, directionless, and all-round-clammy?
And the incuriosity of fog is beyond everything.

There are times I want to go back to somewhere like
 beginning.
The concept of a cell is too advanced for what I want to be,
 sometimes.
Words are cellular, and baulk at it: fog is not-saying.
Fog engulfs. Devours, with no process. Fog is instead of.
Fog extends. Fog bulks. It is nothing you ever see in profile,
 yet there . . .

What is *there*? I put out my hand. Is that a handful of fog?

Does it flow through? And can I expel it with a willed
 clenching?
Or invite it with nebulous fingers, tendons in concert – the
 hand half-opening?

Mind revving up to understand, body boggling
at the falling to inorganic, the going nerveless;
both fall short, bailed up on recognised borders.
The true photograph of fog would disappear,
its corners sucked into monochrome lack of point.
And the drawing of fog would be made with
horizonless sky and land for a pencil.
And the poem of fog would fold
round the wire-thin word *today-as-usual*

all the sounds, ideas of all kinds of being
in a more than pastoral silence.

The man as fog does not bear thinking of.
Green though the slopes are, after.

I displace fog, yet it is inward with me.
I can't do fog. Never, perhaps, to be done with it —
exhalations from a deep place, earth-rumours
fragile and huge, a beauty of a threat
there's no dealing with.

# Reconnaissance

There, circling the lone
river-flat heaped with clean fill –
mounds rough as tipped
but laced with flowering weed:
the water-bird.

Crawling wide, hush the engine.
Mess or no mess
he picks a way in, unfussed,
grey, private, fastidious.
White-ringed, the eye

stares over hummocks, atop
poisings and levellings of his neck.
Towards a nest, perhaps,
his spindle legs course
dead tangles

on the dumped muddled loads
and obstinate chance-set growing things.
His black nib startles to a pause –
adjusts to slant lower –
dots and adds;

then suddenly he's off into wilderness,
seen across brown fern
gadding, urbanely curious
in the city of his desolation.
And is gone. I move on.

# Changing the subject

I thought I had come to see the car,
a sports, all its get-up-and-go
line and shine
gone –
the gesturing bars
that held a windscreen once,
bulldozing air,
rusted past rescue –
too abject now, even without sun,
for wings to perch upon.

As I came turning down from the road
bumping from rut to ridge
all burred with gravel
to the flat
(maybe the way they dragged it in)
the sports disappeared.
There among dirt skid-marks a green-headed parrot
sidled and skittered in wind
off towards red-hot pokers by the water
I shouldn't wonder.
I discovered that that
was what I had come to find:
the thing that mattered,
jarring
and imperious as orange and green,
that ran off apart in the grass, took its downright way
    without waiting
and commanded the looking at.

# Jellyfish

In languor afloat
I lean, *medusa*,
   on the tides' trail.

And need not waken.
Frontless and faceless
my allargando's
slow going closes
in confrontation:
I countenance all
comers, with pursed mouth,
the not-to-be-prised,
the clenched-on-pulsing,
the veiled-and-behung-
with-eddying-frayed-
fringes-of-tassels
immutable valve;

      I mouthe.
I winnow oceans;
I fill them. Floating

# Bivalve

Conforming right now to the norms
neither of courtship nor teaching
the open side of my face spreads out
the closed side tightens.

If this goes on
my head will be a clam slewed sideways
in all the stew of my sea-bed spaces
and will never sit straight on
such the push and wash of its element.

If you try to get round it
you will only be taken in
by the bland loom of liquid expansions.
On the other tack
there's no open approach to the simple
hinge built round with rock
precisely

and I do not despise it;

the wide side of me there with its undulant plush
expanding exploring incessantly
and its nerve-ends softer than water
shrieking on grit and ululating at ease
is there to supply the fit
of my unprised grip
my quick and holding bit.

One side the drying knot.
The other
the pulsing mass shimmers
to farm its parasite
and silkenly tugs my focal creature tight
in the grotto of blood
to usages of light.

## Manatee

Just the same, the poem of the manatee
will not go away. It keeps inshore,
keeps disappearing in the tale
of sightings, encounters, caresses;
massive habitué, mortally
ready to be flesh, of the lull
and shallows of your Floridian sea-board.

There, daylight balances
in a cup, the manatee imperturbably
forages the river-mouth. Sweet passes
to salt, the measure of sun
and distance to the skim of water,
weed loses count and clouds
the pools, straggling herds-wide;

whose people, sinking slowly
to pasture, improbable as Zeppelins,
have never been told what happened
to Steller's sea-cow, two centuries
and an ocean away. Nor asked, what
survives here? Things that lie still,
things that have cover, the armour-clads,

what man lets be. This surely, this
interval, no-man's-land, weed-crammed
sand-bottoms, weed-streams, weed-seasons
and the calm exemplary nation
of lump-faced eaters of weed
browsing, suckling, circling
weedways of visionary twilight.

Poem, boulders that drift,
submarine idyll, silences
incomprehensibly large!

Here come the divers, bubbling
their little quick land-words, working
the frog-feet they learned to reach you,
juggling weed-trails and historic emotions;

they goggle — the mermaid bears
into focus. The death of sailormen's
an undesigning body, after all:
huge-pored, hare-lipped and bald,
the stare one weed-thought, the hide
an aged impervious tolerance
of weed, hide, hands . . .

What did they see in her, those press-ganged
years of pemmican and the lash?
Fresh meat in parting foam —
good men jumped in and the wake
unrolled to tent their feast;
man-eater for sure. The creature's
researched now, re-conceived,

civilised and cast in a cattle-part
for our old crepuscular dream
of man and the peaceable monsters.
Only, men hardly learn
undersea purposes, and course
circuits of deluded will
dandling the enigma; to end

with utility, Midlands farmers
in a Stubbs, dwarfed by their stud
uncaring bulls. The manatee
ignore curious glass,
move against the little limbs
assured of their region, torpidly
hand-feed, and never think to bite.

# Poems drowning

Every day they drown in dozens
clawed down, or land throttled
trailing the venomous deadlines.
They clog my cracks
they die by inches
day rises and quivers
and rises and is unaware.
In the end there is nothing left of them.

But you, poem,
sighted so close to surfacing,
you I will have out
if it's by the hair;
yes this one, alive
or nearly –
by assault or guile
by the feet or the hair
or anything handy or even halfway fair.

# Poems fished out

Midnights
I sit in the bath
writing;
dead upright
(you'd laugh)
unseeing and quite asleep.

Poem drafts
and sketches go
slapping down into the drink;
I come to

and have them all out in no time,
childhood ink bleeding.
Blood's better off
— it clots —
and jottings in biro;
but old heartfelt inks
flush and merge
to the touch of sea. Nightly
I dab with towels
at ink-stains, flood-blotches,
the remains of washed-out words,
identify
and encourage survivors
gathering their draggled crowds
— laying out sheets to dry.

# Eskimo occasion

I am in my Eskimo-hunting-song mood,
Aha!
The lawn is tundra   the car will not start
the sunlight is an avalanche   we are avalanche-struck at our
    breakfast
struck with sunlight through glass   me and my spoonfed
    daughters
out of this world in our kitchen.

I will sing the song of my daughter-hunting,
Oho!
The waves lay down   the ice grew strong
I sang the song   of dark water under ice
the song of winter fishing   the magic for seal rising
among the ancestor-masks.

I waited by water to dream new spirits,
Hoo!
The water spoke   the ice shouted
the sea opened   the sun made young shadows
they breathed my breathing   I took them from deep water
I brought them fur-warmed home.

I am dancing the years of the two great hunts,
Ya-hay!
It was I who waited   cold in the wind-break
I stamp like the bear   I call like the wind of the thaw
I leap like the sea spring-running.   My sunstruck daughters
    splutter
and chuckle and bang their spoons:

Mummy is singing at breakfast and dancing!
So big!

# Water a thousand feet deep
*for Ensor*

I stand washing up, the others have gone out walking.
Being at the best, I am homing in on the worst:

to choke in indifferent waves, over ears in ocean –
skim of earth's sweat – what immensities of salt fear
drench us and tighten – with children to save or lose,
the choice, as from old gods, which to consign to destruction:
how to riddle out waste and defiance? what line cast?
what crying hope hold to? for there is no deciding,
it acts itself, the damning sequence secret
as origin and universe, life as an improvisation
on terrors . . .

the tearaway undertow. But I never lose grasp on my son
or stop swilling plates and setting them to drain;

till blatantly the door. The boy ran ahead of the rest
and is home. I let him in panting, he trails me insisting
Hey, Mum, so close, there is so much floating known here
between us, have we trod the same waters? Hey, Mum,
is there water a thousand feet deep? Yes, I say,
emptying the sink, and give him figures, the soundings
of ocean trenches, which are after all within measure.
As if in the context of fathoms he'd made a mistake
and it mattered.

# Penelope at Sparta

So this is Helen. I used, she says, to be
so fine – such skin, such a waist, a really tiny waist!
her blue eyes looping through wine. She surfaces bewildered,
her fingers flap their exclaimings – she is half-seas over.
And my belly – I was beautiful; my belly, it was white,
    smooth, tight.
Just one baby it took to spoil it, you can't imagine.

She needs no Troy. Simple-stepping Menelaus
has the boys a-shout on the back slope and keeps filling
    glasses.
All she requires is a hearing. Odysseus, she says, Odysseus,
your wife's very clever, very definite. You're a lucky man.
She understands you; anybody can see it.
And I too, going downhill I've discovered I have something
    to offer;
with people, just humanly, I've talents; they say I'm quite
    managing.
I've always known you had depths, impossible to get at,
now you must tell me. You must sit here, on the floor,
come on, I can see it suits you.

Menelaus and I are well-trained, we have that in common.
I sit at my handwork through the harem visit, archaically
    smiling at intervals, making small-talk with some kind of
    house-friend.
She's got him facing her now, his back is somnolent,
heavy with uncritical contempt. From getting no depths,
she's progressed to getting no sense. His mind slowly sorts
tools, weapons, cordage, decking, bartered for in foreign
    places.
Her hand on his shoulder, she's thrashing about re-living
(blonde hair cleaving and parting) her divine self,
her daringly innocent prime. He's past seeing it.

Ithaca has nothing like it. Of course we pleaded harem
against the nuisance of molesters. But now with my son
    in charge
women of rank as well as peasant women
go about free-striding, frank in talk and enticement.

I sit with crochet, as long since, keeping an eye on it,
seeing it through. Unexceptionable. Till in the minutes
of absence and opposition, his turned back and unmoving
    head
blank as sea-swilled crags to her rudderless veering
– from her wheedling to her argumentative –
I sense the depth of rock, wind-fed with privateers,
that I shall never speak of, and he half-forgets;
those years of shores, send-up of the long-resolved landfall,
the crews and peoples, quaysides and stranger hearth-
    welcomes
where sacred above droves of men he embraces, most
    honoured,
the ancient royal witch of her bitter island –
beast-attended Circe bronze-eyed, with strong ankles,
his one-time Aeaean woman.

# Borges at 73

Bone. No finality, but a frame.
The nose drawn up towards bone.
Hand, pen, tongue retreating
into bone. Into the depots of Borges.

Before bone, coral. Reefs, tempting sea-level.
And peopled, in myriads, on principles
to be approached by induction. Look!
they are out in the pool behind you, green on red.
And up, two pools ahead. Only here,
with your sandshoes wet through, scuffing the lapping
wash in the island's lee, coral looks one substance,
uninhabited.

Be still. Examine narrowly, without stooping or speaking.
O richly-caparisoned polypi!
insatiable vortices, treasury of sensors!
utterers of intolerable mathematics!

Their eyes enlarge fragile caverns.
With their corrosive unidentifiable
jelly that is metal that is flesh,
they abolish not-seeing.

In Borges' skull of an assymetrical lemon,
an urchin labours this terminal course
of convolutions. Until (if ever) the catch flicks,
to set at large the implied time-bomb's
seedless interior.

Borges is drying out like a drowned volume,
so many select libraries written
in its margins and over its end-leaves,
and metaphysically crossed with the printed text
which is both previous and simultaneous.

So many libraries unwritten
stock the mere odour of its binding
partly surviving sea-water's
necessary passage.

From his submarine institute,
precisely oriented to oceanic rages
amid its eminence of reef,
Borges is about to transmit
deciphered portions of arcane
memorabilia:

(The transmissions are curious but brief, and there is always the question of the identity of the sender. Constantly they touch on the twin opposites, alike impossible, of a concept never foreshadowed in the history of thought, and of annihilation.

This message appears to come from a different transmitter. The source has been traced to a similar pre-oceanic depth where, at the top of the darkening slope of continental shelf, the debris of light's forcing-ground — the relics of habitation — yield to the abyss.)

In the reception-room of the poet and architect Shashu Hsin-Feng, mother of twin philosopher-princes and seventh Empress of the incestuous blood-royal of Outer Chu-Shu'an a century before it was dragged at the hooves of Ghengis Khan's stallions, she caused to be sunk into the pavement an extraordinary elliptical stone basin. In the waters of this pool she satisfied her curious taste for bestiality with turtles — those living topographies, that figure our shield-shaped skies turned away from us, interacting in dark complicity with a soft underside of Earth. The scene of her copulations was completely lined with a mosaic so richly devised, so skilfully contrived of silver, coloured stones and precious gems, many of which no longer have a name in any language spoken today, that much-travelled connoisseurs have not scrupled to call it the most perfectly intricate in the world.

Nightly Borges removes from it one tiny tessera, each time a different one.

Without fail, the gap reveals a further pattern, so marvellous that it makes the first mosaic (with that tessera removed), although the germ of the second-discovered one, and its primary disseminator, a mere indistinguishable fragment of a motif in the new, huge and probably infinite design beyond; unless indeed the removal of one of its tesserae should permit a glimpse of yet more majestic and complicated perspectives. This last is a feat Borges has constantly in mind, but will never know whether he has at last actually performed.

Through the gap of one tessera, the waters purified by virgin priests for the notorious impieties of a degenerate woman drain, leaving not one drop; Borges' constant removal of the tessera is the means whereby the universal symmetry is nightly bathed in the liquor of the Empress's pleasures. Whether the Empress Shashu Hsin-Feng knew of his visits is not recorded in the surviving five books of her reflections on history, found inscribed on turtle-shell, still less in the popular saying on love which tradition has ascribed to her, and which is all that remains of her atrocious carnality.

# Water life
*for David Albenda*

The Adirondacks, last week of the season;
blue air pausing, car windows sink at wish,
tree patterns weave in water, time for the gleam
of scissors on rock, laid open by flight and ready there
unrusted, seventeen feet down in brown lake water.
Later, warmer and nearer, at a step, at a dip
minnows and their dark-dart twins browsing in mud-shallows
– a finger, a shoe-tip – they shake like filings to a magnet,
governed. The wandering-lilied bay sighs,
that was not its way, and resumes them to lake courses.
But summer weekenders are reaching for wallets and bags,
all cars turn east and south. Ice moves nearer
as the race of lake-men start to the change of season.
The corpse under the cliff-wall mumbles her tale
of tied arms and flesh detained and eight-foot hair
fed on a cleft of the lake-bed thirty years,
who would now be an old woman. Whose college made out
on a query, a fiction, whose students never fathomed
her stirrings, a grotesque mermaid given to brown
wintering of wars and a billion more punctual lives;
who was slime at a breath, her water-miracle surrendered.

I wonder about water-lives. I question the face
that waited half-young while those who had known it young
met it in musings of old age. I swim the parasite
hair-wave lengthening into legend, I try if a slab
of water keeps off memory or holds down longing.
Out of timeless three hundred feet you expect a death,
the remainder. The end to air and earth questions,
the body found, the one-time lover met.
Drag all you will, the water-woman grows
monstrously sinuous amid her monstrous tide
of clues threaded with all the pawnshop past.
What sort of life she's wanting, who can tell?

but she's persistent. What to want of her —
there she drowned, and everything they dredge up
to settle by way of air and earth piety
has never left the water. The hair still feeds.

Time to move on, to bless the innocent water
and blueberry pie pavilions of holiday air.
Wave to old Whiteface, whose big toe nudging lake-caverns
quivers no distrust to his sky-thought head,
his ice-scored rock-fall sides. Drop the clover tassels,
pick up the shoes and go, to ride exclaiming
in the last boat-load of the afternoon
the summer-fallen rapids of a river chasm
and cross the plains, to dine in Montreal.

Delivered, with log-blunt paws of a troll-faced boatman
gouging his pine-green region for anecdotes:
more than you meant to show me at Lake Placid.

# *Shadow on Glass*

1974–1978

*Loved image*

# A photo of me in which I do not appear

So that's how I look:
paths in a park,

a zig-zag of sunshine
tipped so the two women

heading east on the level
walk uphill

obliquely away.
Set piece I'd say,

and trite:
one dark, one light.

## The night

All my childhood night I fell
and fell into the black hole;
I should understand
now my daughter wakes nightmared,
babbling with dread.
I hold her hand.
It's easy to see I'm forty.
I find words, words.


## Now I start to print

Now I start to print —
with lino fifteen by fifteen
or a wood-scrap from Fabio's bench
any size it comes, squared off.
Ink up, dress the block in paper.
I embrace with the pulp of hands
my warm, ridgy, particular
indelibly black child.

# Kin

Kin, the one cloud
high in a far
doorway of clear
evening over the mountain;

and I that sit
dusk-gathering here
with doors ajar,
waiting for night to drift on in.

# The double

Evening, and light makes off.
I take leave of myself. Give me your hand.
Here I stay, standing at the window
watching myself leave;

unrest I've harboured all day
takes up with the dark. In here,
out there, doubt and self-doubt
inhabit, merge.

## Epigram

On the bed, in a line beside me:
manuscripts. No way to sleep.
So I read: a poem of contempt
for women who sleep with manuscripts.
(Seems to think he'd top them in interest.)
He'd get top marks in my book
not for sex or a sermon, but shelving.

## The daily round

We begrudge them, life-long cadgers:
gut to be refilled
the bed remade
the greeting-at-a-distance renewed;
only when Atrox
gorges tripes in the street, we offer
nibbles to the little oppressors –
pious rehearsal, our consolation.

# Wife alone

Bread and water
prison fare
is how I cater
when you're not there;

bread and water
sobering diet:
seclusion order
sloth and quiet . . .

With you not here
I can play martyr
dully preferring
bread and water

to mangled savouries
sweets and wine
I set for your sake,
you eat for mine.

# At the corner of my eye

The shoulder-bag
slung on its doorknob
jerks
a little white dog
with rabid teeth
at me.

My car's
uptilted bucket-seat
stiffens
a stranger hulk
as I lean in
beg pardon . . .

Yes, night's
likelihood
on the lit room
starts
tide without turn
at an eye's rim.

# Sequence

You don't see why I should start
at your sudden foot
in the doorway. So

you frown and snarl with annoyance, which
should scare me; but it is
a reaction. So

my shudder warms to wheedling,
to a laugh. I greet you,
my broken solitude.


# À la carte

Riding high, flapjack,
relapsing always to burn
raw side down on the hot spot;

or the treadmill squab
roast, the martyred allover
everturning other cheek —

your choice of human
hurting, and human hungers.
Going down au naturel

like oysters, saves you
suspense, process, use: the brute
short cut. Not recommended.

## After

Not the first time,
finding it's after
rising from bed and lover
you feel such lust;

as Lucifer at God's
great light so shone,
the angel! and radiant and proud
went out, and then

felt how it was in him
to shine. And if
it felt like this, it was hell
and no heaven enough.


## All OK?

All OK, the walls are bloodless,
the door does not scream
even when you close it,

in the mirror's half-healed wound
the one vase centres
a stub of air.

The holy grain of floorboards
cowled under carpet
avoids the foot.

OK, so the house knows.
So the pictures stopped falling.
You think you can put a date to it?

# The eye swims

The eye swims. Its struggle
is triumphant language. I
for instance was always intent
on surfacing ah for survival
and leisurely rounds of the pool.
Though a glancing turn will pump you
deep too, down spills of sun.
But I never got the knack of sprinting —
the motorized stab, the correctly-angled
ahead-of-its-own-commotion
blade-sweep closing with distance;
now what can I do in this welter
of a cheap pun? front up blind to the black
other side of atmosphere. Blink water.


# Carrying a candle

A hand lifts. Oceans of the dark go
shifting, still our floor fills,
still heads fly menace, the night-fuelled
airship — the move across ceilings
and their spiritless gist of light-bulbs,
the nudge at sidling curtains
vainly impressed with innocent
day-fruits, the lengthening into corners.

The hand steadies, and the dark.
Flame, the prime mover,
reaches to lick a face —
drawn to the night behind
the eye that courting shadow-play
counters the original spark.

# Body and soul

In sleep the soul hangs upside down,
clinging to the body only by its big toe.
                         — Eskimo tradition

*Body*

Night-march. Something deserts me.
It is hanging by a bone
and snickers like a led horse
docile but doubtful of humans.

This is eclipse. Shadows
make off unobserved, oh,
everywhere — up walls, through walls,
riding sills, circling unlit lampshades.

Only my importunate big toe's
unconsciously vulgar tilt
snags soul like silk: off, off but not
too easy, and not quite yet.

*Soul*

Sleep. Have I ever dreamt that
was me — the slavemaster hulk?
Moments of less vigilance
I look for ways out, my own life.
The pinhole in the condom, as they say.
The lip of the mountain lake.
Halfway over, humped silvery
on the crescent ridge, I remember
the valley's form, mine, a life's work.
There has never been anything else.
And my fraying skein crowds back
more than lakes will. Or wings. I alight.

# Exit the lamplighter

Impossible to have darkness ever
close over Clifton Hill's line-up
of best and fairest, photo-
             electric street-lamps;

hard, there, to keep track of the Milky Way
but the Wayfarers maybe keep track by
these gangling intelligences, nightly
             shadowed into shining;

nocturnal birds starve in their sleep
and the total eclipse was a failure
all over Fitzroy, blanched
             under ticking fluorescents;

after sunset the streets practise passes –
they'd give your lamps obedience lessons.
At world's end when the sun goes off
             they'll come on.

# Game

Singing inside the century
under the city's wire-web
singing on criss-cross bus-routes
inside schedules

singing to the blind skylight
under the cloud-screened mountain
singing under the blanket

is red worlds, is inside
warm as two imp daughters
all rolled up in the bedclothes'
ticklish havoc and huddled
singing under the blanket.

# A shadow cast on glass

Coming into the lit room, late
to see a twig laid crossways against glass
where no tree was —
held in the faint glare of a rainy night's
street-lamp unseen for head-high sill,
the grey weightless touch
betraying not at all
how far, how frail the original,
the twig in muted light
impeccable,
the one leaf steady.

# *Mudcrab at Gambaro's*

1975–1979

*Mudcrab*

# Legends of the Nevado
*for Fabio Rodriguez*

   — Always, besides, there was the mountain.
We could not go to make coffee, watch weather coming,
or water the maize-plants in tins on the verandah
   without looking for the mountain.
The tap leaked worse, the skylight panes streaked over
with rust and weed-stains, fleas bit and mice didn't,
the landlady's paraffin stifled and her cigar sickened us,
a woman there wept and screamed odd times all
of an afternoon, the fence keeled over by the lulo
and avocado and the tree of the white trumpet-flower.
   Still, above us, the mountain —
gentlest of obsessions — abode in two climates,
inside us and beyond; beset us, drew us with twinning,
when the high doors stood latched, when massed clouds drove
between and across, inward against our city,
or foundered in level drifts high on the páramo.
When the cathedral cut out and the school pines bestriding
mist came alive with bird-voices, then mountain
breathed and moved closer, hung where it swirled whitest
at house-corners. Blue dawns, it held the east. Moonlight,
glare of a dim eye out of the cordillera.
In the silent dark it gleamed upon no sense, yet
(humped under flashes of the Scorpion's tail,
alert to a snow-shrugging crater's sulphurous throbbing)
shaped us precarious continents of night.
   Constantly we make for the mountain;
shaken in a huddle, through green precipitous foothills
from maize to grass to flowers in the lee of rocks
and lichened posts. Soil to sand to rock.
The air turns sleet. The water-course, sand under mist,
sodden the colour of dried blood. Not knowing which
death it is waits in the meeting: death of the mountain,
death of the amazed vision. Must I lose my eye
or mountain give up its spectral persistence?

That time the mountain had its honour,
a tyre and the gradients connived. We did sign on
with a mountain-man in the sand-dunes, his visitors' book,
and gave it best. And fell back on our verandah
only to hire a jeep and a short-sleeved driver
who refused a coat and drove us straight to the crest
past the main turn-off, El Triunfo, La Esperanza,
the fourteen bends in sand, the streaked volcano,
sentinel ridges and the thatched final Refuge.
Wind, whiteness, what more to say, the Nevado
is there still, blue scarved round its snow-shoulder;
my mountain too. Met without collision,
nodded each other's air, and correspond
in Andean space the soul remembers. I lean
over photographs, straighten a gangling furred mountain
flower, take breath in the vultures' balance of flight,
don't need photographs. But have puzzled over the year's
festival, journey, vision, that lives there; this
for all unriddling: I am born to one continent,
I marry another. As near as I'll get to the mountain.

# Family

In my mother's family
We have no ancestors
only the long silence
between pogroms.

In my father's family
we have little tradition —
lands, legends, powers
passed us by.

In my country
we have no grandparents
no continuing song
no dances. Silence

feeds music,
father's our legend.
Husband and wife, estuary
into a continent,

we open our arms:
touch peaks, touch breakers.
Forest and white water
our children dance.

# Old friends

Away from them, you angle
to retrieve their faces. Their tastes lurk
in your household habits,
in their talk
the past runs to kiss you. And there's
the you you'd forgotten,
with long hair
and uncertain opinions.

For if, past forty,
it's hard
to call them debonair —
still, like the worst reporter
last on the crowded phone, they cared
once. They were there.

# Writing a biography

Hiding the mirror with a map,
hoping the mirror-lady'd stay lost,

I set to charting a century-long
overview of the subject:

gulfs, roads, the early farmlands.
Why they came, how they worked, what they saw.

But my left eye comes boring through
at a salt-pan. The right dangles

by the watercolour crater-lake, poised
over adolescent eruptions:

and hey! there's my heroine, double-crossed
under shadings for height and highways

once cart-wide, wheel-deep in grass.
Winds are unburying her, floods

scouring her mud habitation,
jumbling land-divisions and date-lists.

It hasn't the look of a woman.
I unhook the map. Meet the mirror.

# The piano on the beach

*Surely it is inconceivable*
*(thus the thinker, venturing on deck)*
*that a New World*
*owns less*
*than its original!*
                    Kris Hemensley, *Meanjin* 1/1976

Music, yes, adorns the colony.
The Germans, even on Sundays, sing.
We girls all play
or would,
the piano propped in sand

where Alfred twisted his left ankle.
In gales of sun the salt-caked keys jar
to the long swells
irr irr
rah clanking rah rah rah

Here, insects beat nearer than the sea,
there's axe and churn, wheels, dogs barking. And
Matthew slips out
the flute,
any time he's this way.

Strings do for snares, sides for a fowl-pen.
Not that there's luck in them. Making do
and moving on
inland,
we'll think of ordering.

## Palais de danse

And my aunt Bets
always the bright one
sulked off to London
shows with the rest;

Grandma hoping
she'd find a nice boy
forget the goy and
throw him over;

but not a hope.
They all trailed back
and Betsy married
her glib oboe,

then went and sweated
in Foys' selling furs
to buy a divorce.
Grandma was dead

young, whom Grandfather
never helped at all
from his orange-orchards
at Petah Tiqva,

her girls turned sad
and her samplers lost
stitched by the Volga.
To a jazz piano

the 'thirties drove over
Bets and the others
and the tide came up
on the beach at Cottesloe's

years of fox-trots
where Bets had her band
in the Palais de danse
now gone from the rocks.

# The big girl

I walked to the teacher's room
the music under my arm,
and the big girl striding met me —
I thought no harm.

Her hair was bright on her head.
Her shallow eye was steady.
"Want me t'slap your face f'you?"
I saw no remedy.

She slapped, and a life of lessons
fell with the music down.
She yanked out each page and shredded it
strewn on the ground.

I saw how my playing ended
and I heard how daylight said
my name in the stride of a stranger
and the eyes in her head.

# I've always wanted a brass dodo
*for Sibila*

It frisks in a girl's hand,
little pet, the whale
she bought for the cant of the tail,
the glide
of fingertips on brass
and look! her own gold face
melting and remaking along the fluent side;

decent she feels, reminded
you shouldn't hunt them
and if men do, whales haunt them
in museums.
Busy Taiwan's
buoyant upon these dollars;
maybe a whale's still blowing. *Carpe diem.*

# And behold, it was very good (Genesis 1.31)
*for Rebeca*

Draw me a crocodile    make him a gentleman
What a nice tail now put a    ribbon round his neck and
how about a giraffe    remember he has long legs as
well as a long neck Oh those    are good spots
give him a tree poor thing he just    can't get the grass
that's right now what's that?    well if it's a dog where's the
ears and do give him    meat in a little pot let's
see do you think a cat    a cat that could be friends with
that dog goodness looks like a    rabbit never mind just
give it a tail    give it one that curls ah a
bow that's pretty and now    how about some birds the
top looks kind of empty    ?

# Cooker for the rubbish-tip

The streetward vista a sight less docile:
our front door blocked outright and us fended
off by that once-white automaton
of an untradeable cooker its iron flaps lightly
up and consentingly shut maybe
cemented by gravyfat effluvia and who
will manhandle remove it should could or
might? garbos and Minister of course
intend is involved concerned misunderstood
mindful of the community's mandate and
if you (mate) manage a youngish obedient
machine it is certainly, before it is too waste
family soul and etcetera wise, food
for thought, the malice of your old has-been.

# Clearing a cupboard

What shall we do with it, dear, momentoes of the failed
marriages and births? It's all very well to closet
debris – greasy tins embossed with cheek-to-cheek bells,
and silvered place-names; and salt away wedding-portraits
unsampled, unguarded in albums – sharper than the rest.
No, keep the bootees, for babies that promise to live;
we've learned not to give on spec. Experience of waste
suggests that our memories, even, should be tentative.

Now here's this white-ribboned favour "De Hernan y Rosmira"
from a land where, good god, the church-wed can't divorce.
They'll be listed together (tableau!) in heaven. Familiar,
these candid snaps from the years of kids and visits;
the starring mini-smiles look like mine and yours . . .
souvenirs! they'll bury us; out. So much less to get rid of.

# The line of tearing

You ask what I'm at, tearing
wearable denim for rags. But
it barely held, tight on fat, had it.
Serviceable, you said? The dye goes –
meant to – and now the very weave's come
unstuck. No straight up and across
failing; twill effect, right side
thinks it has a right to the left,
fights all the way down, teasing out
strain-shapes. And why just there –
creasing? pants jagged on a car-brake?
or just 87 agitated washings . . .
there's a weakness in every pair.
Takes time to show where, and tearing.

## Is it poetry? they ask.

                                              Is it really
poetry? Sometimes by the fireplace
(and there'd been a fire, no mistake)
Ellen asked, is it still alight?
We'd peer at the whitening flakes
and chunks paled round a black stump.
It helped if you switched off the lamp.
Outside would be clearer, grass
and scrub and fences and tree-tops
roaring and blazing miles-wide
and fire-fighters awed in witness.
On the widening scale, sun and stars
are the only proven poets.
But their language deserts them, the warmth
of this and the light of that.
So many that have been, known
by these we see — light-years back!
And alas, the contemporaries our children
will reproach us for not deducing.
Back to the impatient questioner,
the poet, this warmable hand,
painted shutters and doorbells of the skull
swelling or clacking in weather,
and our strange inhabitant puzzling
warm or cold? Is there anything out there?

# A line of notes
*for Ensor*

Stranger than greeting my own
writing from the mail-box,
sitting at the piano to a paper
from a hand not mine;

today untrumpeted someone
trying it over
pencilled a row of notes here.
My racy son

who strummed, tried it on once, what *good*
is music? and I told him
what you tell them — same old things —
what I could —

like the dumb need music ails,
for us; and the brutal
programme we're fed into, for music.
Speaking of souls

the big-head embryo crotchets
tune me to him, each
to others, the meeting and feast
and entire opera.

# An odd voyage
*for David Malouf*

        My room had been joined on
                              so long
housedust was thickening the ink.
                              So I cast adrift
my little red cabin (so long!)
                    all lights on.
A skyful of waves gliding
                        played at flight
on the ceiling,

        We nosed out through
                        nasturtiums
northerly.
     There it was: the inland sea
explorers' tongues baked for.
                            Its blue was gamesome
with lake-dragons roused
                    to lick bows. No-one about.
Mists scarved in the grove,
                    poles marking shallows;
some sprouted leaf,
                the blue-water-rooting trees
olive, and jacaranda, and the shrub
                        bayberry.
The island tufts
        held guaduas creaking,
plumed heads signalling on
                    to sunken tops,
curuba
     laced across rocks, fruiting . . .
     and there were
                    birds:

provident pelican,
                  dawn-honking snowgoose
high and far, one
               companionable vulture
above, attending for death
                    and scraps. For I tell you
this was a human voyage. A scarlet
                                cardinal
perched windward
            on the rail, out from land,
winged like the angel,
                  who I now perceive
commended me
          to chinoiserie and the quattrocento.
The deck had taken on
                a little motion
and glitter
       of water in the bilges
    when a clock
             hove, tick-tock,
alongside.
       Time
    struck,
         it seemed, for something;
so I moored. I had not
                crossed concrete yet
but the appointment
              was on tarmac, with agenda.
When I came to re-embark
                    the sea had all gone back
to whatever galaxy . . .
                  My craft had drifted by habit
to the old dry-dock, and gracious!
                          dust and ashes!
A very little pile remained,
                    nails from picture-frames,
the linocutters of course
                burnt handleless.

The typewriter must have been
                         of use to someone —
no sign of it. But a spiky wink
                         from the rim
of the maw
         of Emily's silver dinosaur;
I started in reflectively to clean it
                         of soot —
foot jarring
         a lamp (the lightless parts) . . .
The children stood
             a bit uncertain:
      well thank goodness
                         you weren't
in it, and what is there for dinner?
                         all the apples are gone,
Dad's downstairs.
             Hi, I said, it could be worse
and maybe I'll teach you about boats.
                         I got this one to float,
nobody much out there this time,
             still, there will be.
Plenty of room on board;
             we could look at the sea-bed
they tell me in colder hours
             is bones, bones.
Maybe we could fly too . . .
             Trouble is, getting in and out quietly.
The steering's a dream, it's the fuel;
             could we run her on music?

## Isadora

Come the machine-age, I'm one sweet
look here guileless trans-
oceanic artiste yielding
more than stones'
classical, the word is simplicity,
no swathed turret, my silk borders
flutter from the clasp, a heavenly
simper, body

yes, luminous von Thode undid
nothing, his spry St Francis, I flipped,
a Santa Clara for Bayreuth. Vowing
breasts, astral flights, a high-bourgeois season's
heart-streaming scarves, any minute now
watch my wheels!

# Madrigal

Walking down through woods
neither of them idling knew
names for the flowers in bloom.
Songs they trailed in the dark paths,
each his own song.

That time they stood by the water
it was not themselves they saw
but leaves moving, shadows, scum.
Light was going from the water
and gone the swan.

# Replay

Summer was tales of children
to an autumn air –
the lovers that leaf-heavy summer
dreaming lost children

called out among leaves, to wake
and rehearse each night
*you're doing very well, keep at it . . .*
The nightmares did,

the pleaders, the wanting to feel
beautiful, beautiful!
And where does it take them?

Back to the children
impaled on their terrible game:
who will play, who won't.

# Soldier's gravestone, Kalemegdan

Here's a Jugoslav naive
sculptor with a problem:
where to put the gun.

It's regimes lay out money
and generals the men;
here mallet and chisel record
the gun's obsession —
they started an arm and a gun
and draw the conclusion.

The gun goes through the arm
mouthing its loverlike
stone word:
                flesh      flesh

# Tutorial

Let's be frank: duplicity's fun.
Small outlay and moderate exertion.
It's addictive, mind you, with hidden
expense when you expand operations.
At the end of a short course in duplicity
you try the whopper – they all do –
suddenly you're driving four-in-hand
with three at least gone over the cliff.
Well, I ask you, what did you want,
integrity or experience? Skill's
one thing and success is another.
Learn from failures! that old chestnut –
keep succeeding or you won't be around
to be skilful. Alternatively
you won't have anything left
to be skilful about. Hang on
to your seat, hang on to your investment,
and with any hands left over
hang on. Let go of the rest
when anything you grab answers.
Remember most of you are losers.
Winners can throw away the course-notes.

# Mudcrab at Gambaro's
*for Tom Shapcott*

At Gambaro's, we are fearfully pleased
to light on land-agents in threes
and fours for lunch.
They check us for affluence
and return to their talk.
Well, and so the Big Boy's coming back —
did he tie it up?

Conducted, placed,
we toast the midday feast.
Morning's boom holds up,
zooms into the order of mudcrab.
You pour, you tumble
ice, you burrow the bottle. I tipple and wonder
how light's wine-colour.

The pallid easy oysters
pass, precursors
to here it comes! the roseate big'un!
platefuls of plated pincers,
shanks, joints,
every one neatly smashed, our own Big Boy,
heaped up high.

We eat, ingenious and attentive.
The land-agents breathe heavily.
Among tables, through the room
grave women come
gathering greaves,
flanges, splinters we forced with hands bleeding —
devotees

of smooth encapsulated
flesh, the tingling white
of beachsand at daybreak.
Staggering, the land boys push back
their dogged chairs.
Mere steak. They diminish sweating in the late-lunch glare.
We are mudcrab, and air.

## *The subject*

Most subjects are dead
before you take them
up. If you're lucky
it's only till
you take them up.
Perhaps because of
the sideways scuttle
mudcrab's not over-
paeaned, stays alive
right up to the pot where
you take and toss him
into hot water
and by this the poem's
out of its depth
getting hotter . . .
the pained ladies
are not informed,
they pry into his vesture
guiltless but let
just one of them guess
the ardour −
even at table
as we leant over
a mandible jiggled

the ladies flushed
for all the world like
well what about the subject
still kicking minutes
or moments (reader)
after you've
taken it all in?
I tell you honest
some we lit are jumping
flambé
a thousand years on.


## *An upbringing*

      I have come home to you and mudcrab.
Never inclined to put off, to keep expectation polished,
always a gulper and gobbler for present titbits,
a gabbler they slowed over years of rebukes and debating,
I am learning now what presenters kept dinning in vain:
there's a thing I have starved half a lifetime for, ignorantly.
A word for it, my preferred and penultimate term for it –
    mudcrab.

All my childhood the high mystery of mudcrab
– charred Rousseau angel, volant, with French horn –
hung above Sunday early, the way to the Broadwater.
We'd be putting away single peanuts, sighting
milestones in the left-hand grass. Dad knew them all.
At this creek, or was it the other, there'd be talk
of yabbying, shadowy mangroves to seaward, and mudbanks
of the legendary and incomparable mudcrab,
denizen of sucking shallows and dark silt tideflats.
And what hints of the wild-man guile of the getters of
    mudcrab!

Ritual meat, it was not for children or tennis-friends.
It was laid in, by the ritual half-dozen, for Big Boss from
 Stockholm,
who missed out on two lots — six swelling the boot of the
 Holden
and six in containers, pinched for space, in the fridge.
In the end, containers and all, mudcrab rose
apocalyptic on mornings of heat
to rout us from house and car and land, appalled.
Mum swung the door, Dad ran with Courier'd mudcrab
stretched five-arms'-length off, later hosed the boot,
and we closed every single back window tight for cloudless
 days
before trying to do something with the bin. The curse of
 mudcrab.

So misguidedly, on a birthday shout at Lennons',
parents' friend footing the bill, I flouted for foreigners
the homeshore mudcrab. On from caviar — Dad demurred —
to Bombe Alaska in its chocolate carapace, cocking
a green-toffee butterfly, roaming crimson jelly,
spilling its Sundae guts of fruit-salad and ice-cream.
The great mudcrab shrugged his shell and went back down
 his hole.

Growing up. One way of putting it: dodging mudcrab.
The years of "austerity" when the Best was desperately
 still-and-always
British, for pleasure read principle, the luxury of high art
held for questioning, a migrant with un-Australian habits.
And mudcrab was hiding out in the creeks down the bay.

Sundays we shook sand off in the car. Cubbies tottered
from the sheer weight of bougainvillea, we sang God Save
and marched into school. The Anglican canon who bored me
came on from baptising you. In a decade of previews
you pre-swam your adult races in State championships
at the Baths, for God, King and Grammar. Time told decades.
Students, we walked rank corner lots, backyards, beaches,
fiercely desiring the life-and-death elegant decisions
of taste and need. Restless in glazed verandahs
medical students played Bach, on Breakfast Creek houseboats
rocked stacks of Bessie Smith 78s, there were curries and
    Fellini,
Anouilh and brandy-parties. Antique-dealers suffered
from the avant-garde, it came under Tastes, Acquisition of,
entrée to the feast. Smug mudcrab puttered with nippers
in the wet-sand evening breeze. You grew up
and I did, in cities of the steaming river-plain, and both
fell into the middle way, here and afar. More wonder
that, created by those fifties, now we move
in the lemon air of precarious middle years
down face-lifted dear steep original streets
homing in lightsome, high and at last, on mudcrab.


## *Occasions of mudcrab*

On a spine of Brisbane sit us, feast-fingered, high,
uplifted, sated, where we sat the course.
Lust has a low reputation, gluttony a worse,
tricked out in flaring euphoria . . . oh, for their good
tenderness, to hold tenderness, invent
the figures and flexible graces for our mortal
consorting in sections of flesh. The easy-to-be-parodied-
for-all-the-seldom-it-happens occasions of mudcrab:

2.

We land at good airports to mudcrab.
Your ring touches mine – mudcrab!
Our eyes stroke cheeks hair (mudcrab,
someone is jotting a catch on the text *mudcrab*).
They can't understand
    why we can't stop grinning over mudcrab!
Your suburb from the back verandah –
    mudcrab entirely,
    and the sad paper of our fleshly letters.
And the Brecht cassette in the dark's
    pinchgut racket
    reels pure high black
    live Brisbane basement midnight mudcrab.

3.

At meat, we are people of mudcrab
seizing a sanctioned haul
in sea-breathing reaches.
Look, the pull's there, white
threading scarlet nippers,
the linkage of tendons
in slick and killing case.
Break, pluck, eat
from the casket displayed
and its elegant flasks.

O the sweet meat.

## *The mudcrab-eaters*

Nothing lovers in their forties do together
    that they don't, you'd say, repeat.
    But then, this day, what others here
    so feast, rising on the lean threat
    of the night apart? or so taste
    and toast their exquisite lot?

    Who else at Gambaro's is happy?
    With dolphin glances serving
    each other, the lovers sit, sea-delight
    lightening air. And though
they night and morning years-long sat down to mudcrab,
    they have never eaten mudcrab before.

## *On going for mudcrab*

If the ancients praised mudcrab, I beg their pardon;
I haven't seen it done.
Pork-crackling, Stilton,
haggis, roast beef, wine —
there may be a rondel on the after-dinner mint.
This time, we dine.

Let's be clear on one thing: I know I've overdone it.
Never could stand watching a stove.
But this gaudy adventure
upon the crustacean notion —
clashing and snapping to keep you on the jump, in magenta —
it takes getting over.

Mudcrab, let's face it, keeps coming out protesting
against being code or shorthand
for the Good Things, for you.
Music now, landscape — they're taught as
good things, there's opera, views, there's trees that would do.
Mudcrab takes forcing,

mudcrab takes time, mudcrab takes place in river-mouths
developers fit with marinas.
Builders there float
their foundations, remark over dinner
the rare revered mudcrab's hard to keep about,
could be nearly extinct.

And the final extension at the Natural History Museum
I humbly enquired of (just
a poor poet, I kept saying,
trying for the facts behind lunch),
offered sand-lobster, flapjack huh! shovel-nosed crayfish, and
    wait for it –
puffed the Balmain Bug

on which I choked. *Scyllaridae* fared no better.
(Them Scyllids can gobble me whole
before *I* come at *them*.)
Southeast Queensland, I howled down the phone,
littoral! spitting gobbets of the Bug, delicate they tell me
but true mudcrab for soul –

to get back to the topic. Why yes, this is a regional effusion.
The thorough Museum down south
has referred my query.
Me, I'm taking the mudcrab path
to you and Gambaro's at noon, where good fools live dearly
hand to mouth.

# Fourteen times saying rain for Tom

After heat, and the hills damply nudging,
rain falls on timely sleep.

The high darkness of Taringa under inkwash sky
is groves for dancers;

wide-eyed streetlamps scatter
and crossings pose blinking, canted among ridges, St Lucia.

Your plants stand open as bowls and alert as retrievers
on the back verandah,

blest spirits revive,
around us the River courses heaven and earth.

The lovers switch on a jiggety radio, low,
switch it off for rain-sounds —

great murmur of rain spreading over suburbs and into the hills
— splashes on a path —

sluicing down the gutter-spout — runnels and drips by the
    louvres —
splatter, a broad leaf.

By a swimming-pool light
the elephant-beetle gleams and fronts up, shirring and
    threatening,

and cane toads flop in the wet,
hands of creation feeling coolness, feeling grass-runners,

or flattened, lie pale to the blackness of rained-on bitumen,
or silt down in dirt roads.

There is not loneliness – your room all round me
drinks sounds of life,

the aluminium plant ailing outside
lifts, unfolds, remakes language,

the mid-air silvery darkness easily, easily
prints thought like touch.

# The line always there

Darkness and rain: an ancient feeling.
Alone, roofed under rain, I stream out

like hair in water. I am here but free,
the River is loosed about our wires and treetops

and fills the dark garden, all things
are held in themselves, are attentive, are night

and have passage. Rain over the railway bridges,
rain over the freeways and on, a light chases rain

and dips in scrub, darkness of the seacoast
by unfooted dunes, white crests running in the thought,

the line always there, slipping and spreading
on, the high point breaking, an equilibrium.

# Witch Heart

1979–1982

Sweetheart

# How do you know it's the right one?

Can you play it on a keyboard?
On one string?
Is it partial to silence?

Can you exalt it
continuously?
Can you debase it?

Can you look at it curdled
and pasty
in the glass after midnight?

And eat it and drink it
whatever —
it with its memories

and malaise, years and days of it?
Must you have it?
Will you love it or live with it?

# Leaving

Call it home.
Some part of woman
did trace its dark corridor
in the bones of children.

Yet it's me leaving,
the milky lights of its night-walks moving in me
and a dough of blood
where I couldn't keep my room —

he'll manage,
whitewash

but I'd rather leave
the grave
the grave

## Leaving the trees


Garden stuff, the honour of trees.
You move out, taking clean bricks,
leave him blocks
of intractable bluestone.
This is the division of mere goods.

But trees are rooted.
The betrayal of flesh goes on.
One afternoon
savoury pepperina's hacked out that would
heave at the house-wall.

Your small things bed down in pots —
begonias, a fern.
Trees remain.
Apricot, plum,
pine, loquat, wattle

promise now as never before.
And your olive, the gift-tree.
The lilac's come good this year
and japonica's frankly
broken out —

was it you stood in their sunlight?
is this what they wanted?
You leave behind
a part of honour,
your trees fruiting.

# Travelling

You cannot leave that old you were
*You are making new*
You cannot open the windows
*You will taste air*

I left myself in walls
They paint them over
I left myself in a garden
They prune hard
They eat
where I doubted and starved
lying straight on the stretcher
by the steel cabinet

You are not in that room any more
*You cannot leave it*
You travel with it folded
like a map

# That house of yours

You can shuffle it off,
that house of yours.
You can wait for the money.
I cannot be indifferent.
It spoke with its poor voice
at the wrong time,
and offered its stair.

It hoped with the tank
in the overgrown backyard.
You never even gave up
your post office box.
You made poems of the spiders
and sub-tenants
and drove off with the pot-plants.

# Homecoming
*for Tom*

Home from the long journey, you bustle.
I lie in your deckchair unable to wake or sleep.
I am being not-here.

There are your children.
They pull at you, they are wind at the involuntary clouds
full of goodness.

They bring you where you empty yourself
and the achng.
It is bounty, it is how you love, it is family.
The shine of it, and the need.

When I wake
there is a drop coming off each leaf
outside your long-curtained window.
The insects begin.

Heat has stopped for today
but not the rain
– only there is this clearing –

I am a child at the window before dinner,
before lights go on.
I breathe
exact shoots in the tangle.

And now broken skies lean through the freshening tree
and now you have come in

we can watch white storms in the gully
knot and wrestle

then over the drinking earth
again
the gathering up.

# The waking

All night the house has swung to our light-light-light
    breathing
almost without a wall, rooms clinging in a last vibration
of the Brahms Capriccio. Now out of the valley's
    no-thought
a pine rises, broods, dreams scour, we are wading shore-
    waters.
Near the piano a frame stares, rooms hive off, scents stir,
the pastels return, by this vines cream the hillside.
All the vegetal presences stand to recognise light
by the garden stair, light stripes the raw slope under.
Remade in light, notes jostle. Particulars are the
    condition
of waking, the snagged floating, bird-call, under sheets
it is your hand, it is the body's inhabitant, it is my hand
    given back,
it is your hand moving. I breathe deep and turn.

# A concerned aerial view

The moody thing a foot is.
Hands have to be clever,
cannot afford sulks,
"expressive" etc. of course —
effleurage and hypocrisy.
But your ground-down pitiful slab
unable, slung on bones,
awarded that immense callus, the heel,
for its earth-bound utility,
beaten up with work
and always at odds with the image —
how is a normal person
to get on with two lowgrade misfits
purple at the end of the bath
and come summer, dirty-shell-white
to your tanned shins?
And the huddle of degenerate toes!
Splay, play with them, they're never
less than conscious, never more
than first stumblers out of bed each day,
unwillingly from Eden. Poor things,
they consider the anemones.
At least as you confront them you think
they've got each other.
Even better, the nightly clambering
back into tree-memory:
I could be eloquent as leaves, they murmur,
feed my root . . .
All this time, the busybody hands
offer the overview, overkill
and totally convertible knowhow
to scoop kicks and the kickback:
I can do everything better
they say, let *me*, let *me* . . .

# The surprise

You open the door next morning
to the shambles the children made of it –
the piano cannot speak
for the orderliness,
meal-places on proffer
books in rank
shoes at attention
table on shine
and the floor's expanse:
it's all quite overcome.
The sofa cushions set up
are nearest to giggling
though the children
are dreaming untidily still
and still to remember.

# Arms race

See this
one colour
fast
jet
and this
all bunched round inside
spider
trade you

want a lemonade
lemonades they're good
brown
they're cokes
watch this
real cool
lemonade
hit
the bacon

soft hit
everyone's got bacons
but bloodsuckers
this bloodsucker got
this tiger
and a beachball
and see this semi
mist

aw semis
bet you haven't
even seen
a jumbo

who cares
jumbos are dumb
like peewees
who wants one

you can maul a semi
just one good tombola
you've got to know
marbles
can't get a good tom
just anywhere
take this
slasher
smooth
watch this
watch it

missed

well the way
you've got them set up
anyone would

anyway
look out
see that birdcage
red
well
this is the big one
dead killer —
look at my tom!

# Drew

Up over Easter.
Place on the river.
Got the dog to feed,
   retriever —
   good boy!

Dish out the side door.
Feed in the tool room.
Spaniel in the long weed,
   now then!
   Here boy!

Hens in the chookyard.
Cows up the back field.
Hollows under high roots . . .
   New here.
   Go boy!

Bolt through burr.
Flicker by fences.
Race down river banks
   no brakes —
   big Drew!

Sluice off, shake-up,
swish like a carwash —
hair all water-swirls!
   Heel boy.
   Sit.

# Canoes

This morning
six red canoes on a trailer
nipped into a side street.

They rode light but firm
six red canoes clamped separately
three each side —

three-decker riverbend turning
left under a tram's bows
in Hawthorn.

## The city workers

Round five the workers of the nation
run roaring into Central Station;
next day from seven until ten
roaring they all run out again.
What poor brute kept behind the door
spends all night teaching them to roar?

# A legal error, 29th March, 1847
*for Zoë*

Catherine and Margaret Hennessey's
hard-spurring tomboy japes
made of them proper menaces,
currency jackanapes

Furiously Riding on Sundays.
*Custody* fell on their fault.
Should have been served with a *Summons*;
that's how the jades did a bolt.

Mayor's court, watchmen and constables
else had committed and tried 'em;
kept breaking Sabbaths, just once to put
paid to their Furiously Riding . . .

Eighteen-forties larrikins,
off they flounced into their lives.
Maybe they scampered and ramped again;
maybe they wore into wives.

Here's to the legal crror
confounding procedure since Genesis —
luck to a handful of helter-
skelter Melburnian Hennesseys!

# Wintering inland
*for Phyllis Webb*

The sea-island woman
is pale and subtle.
Sea-winds drained her.
In the city of mirrors
her face moves unmated.
While she is in the prairie
the mishaps find her –
a spilled glass, a caught finger.
She panics. She is illegally parked.
She will be followed each dark night
of a winter of snow.
Only in halls
under the silk banners high up
where low sun crosses
she stands at the hint of damp wind
in colours of sea-grass,
the shift into rain-slopes
and breathing of great trees.

# Laughter in fall
*for Susan Musgrave*

She needs to be always
in love, they say, laughing
over her latest
escapade —

ruined her husband's
connections, how can a lawyer
let his wife
run off with the defendant?

How can he go on defending
drug cases?
What if Caesar's wife
ran off with some Romanised

barbarian? Who'd trust him?
He'd divorce her.
By then they'd have parted,
her and her lover.

Like this one, who needs to be always
in love, they say laughing,
all of them
needing

something else,
they don't run off
or ruin connections,
who knows why?

They spend time for loving
on bad poems or good poems,
redrafting, recycling.
She's the fall girl,

she does it for them
always
they say laughing
in love to the end of the poem.

# The glove

Nobody takes hands seriously any more.
The days when a homecoming woman half-turned, arching
her buttoned forearm — gone with the scaffolding of
  whalebone.
Never more, surprises of chapped inadequate hands
pulled from anyway decent gloves, nor, unfolding,
the unflurried palms and natural lotus-languor
of paler girls, still, each with a scar or wart
half healed, or lefthand index bitten to the blood.
This you take up, flung on a table in the vestibule —
its pair, yes, by the chair-leg — there's a hand;
kid, soft as the veined inner wrist, curl-fingered,
ridged with oversewn tendons. The gape buttonless.

# Strop

Dad was one for the old times. The good old. On the end
of a bout of old leather, he'd fetch up "one for good"
as good as one for the road, going by the shine
he took to cow-hide and latherings, backhandling his
   moustache.
ARGEE NO. 33, Genuine Hide, Mum tried to,
black lash and brown, she eyed as if they bit,
swingeing carnivores with all their feed-time alacrity
and full-fed high shine that me and Billy sweated at
after. A touch with the hook end was the ultimate threat.
Never got that, myself, till the article came my way
from Dad's girl, worse times, not much she'd still call his,
and her unloading loot for her great step forward
back into circulation. Billy got the Bible
Mum had written us (birth-date, space for marriage) into.
Spur to prick, so to speak, but what girl ever knew Billy
intent? We'd set up the girls, so he'd talk girls,
**come closing time he'd rather fight. Come on, he'd get
   into us,**
mix it! No man'll see my back, and no damn
slut to bottle me, can't you do anything but whore?
Mum never would've believed it. He was the one
got the hook end solid, elder son not tough enough
and not fast enough on the ball, not tall enough ever,
took to his fists too late and anyway guileless.
Lucky coming later, I sized it up, could handle it,
but it's a bad taste when they phone about where he is
and there's nothing will knock him sober. Can't take
   him home.
Now the strop, in good order there where the kids can
   see it –
I always wonder why it never taught him anything.

# Dinner at River Acres

*for Ian Rasmussen*

The salad chopped, the fowl in the pot turned down —
let's go and see Vern before dinner. Your back's long,
Vern's back is long through the fence as you both turn
talking cattle for market. We dangle at the back of the ute
being townies. You come back, you hop in, we all drive on
to the market garden. Zucchini, not as big as last week,
and pumpkins are coming along, beet crisp as wings;
between rows, deadly nightshade stars the ground.
Sprinkler blocked, pump to kick over, give it time —
round the dam, yabbie-lines. Back on the flat, there's Vern
waiting, sort of, and Morris. Through-gate and up-paddock
you're hooting and clapping at the fence, they start, we're
  in second
and Vern too, and Morris with the whip, and the cattle
  likely
to do anything at all, lumbering across in front,
starting from the drummed car-doors, deciding yes,
gate, then no, bracken, and how do we know where the
  stumps,
never mind, keep heading them off. We huddle in the turns
till fast and sullen they flow to the yard's shadow.
You slip down, a few words, the time's yours. We wait.
  Once through
running to shut gates. The rooster burns, back home.

# Funny

The funniest thing in the world:
how it rotted the sill,
burst in the cupboard,
bit her hand,
got at his brain.
Funny things happen.

The funniest thing, how she got there, with her record,
why he did it, after all this time;
and
who was waiting for them.
And as for what they did with the money!

It's a funny world.
And I've heard a phrase, a funny way of putting it:
this driver once,
just had his car polished off
by a semi-trailer; funniest thing in the world,
parked to check the route, wandered off behind a bush for
   a minute;
and once, after family dinner
where no-one spoke a word.
It was the grandmother, I remember, funny woman:
Life's a bit of a giggle. That's what they both said.
People are funny.

They keep going,
there's something dignified about it.
And just when they seem to be getting somewhere
they crack up. If it isn't cancer
it's hoarding cardboard.
Or they get scared
of the doorbell.
It's the funniest thing in the world.

# The night hand

By night, shadows start out between the fingers. They creep into the ravines of calloused knuckles, edge out from the white overhang of the nails and up side gullies to take in even, by a sudden night-leap, half-moons. Each nail gleams, each is new-seen distinct terrain, its shining camber vulnerable to claims, change, ravage.

The thumb has disappeared in a black gulf; four misshapen prongs are the ends of this fish-fleshed enterprise. Darkness that hid in the sleeve all day is quietly, terribly flowing over the monotone boneless veinless skin. Where is the compact, contracting day hand? Its fingers are prised apart with night fingers.

The night hand has designs on light. It will pull up the close-patterned covers, close down day, there now, tomorrow another. The great cover-up.

You hang on to the ridged cuff, the lamp-rim, day-break: these ranges of the night journey, last visible peaks.

Their gaping edges first pucker, and then begin to melt. What if night is out and will never fit back!

Always one for the road, a great packer, you stuff night in behind the flaking greying jumble of the day set, you tell it to stay there, at all events it is too done to rave its old lead parts, it will not appear in the payroll or the handbills.

You trundle on to the next location, the next booking. You have the night hand up your sleeve.

# Halley's Comet
*for Hyman Spigl, astronomer (1911-1962)*

To see Halley's Comet, far-sent

once-in-a-lifetime-faithful
waif of our universe, return
and flaunt her spill of light
kicking her train behind in the curvet
like a flamenco dancer;

to feel an incurious eye cross
worlds, your brow by night,
your sunlit garden, her nearing
slice the blue air of days
till she drops away, shimmering

stream first, light-years backward
in mine-black space, for mantle
distances a lonely child
invokes, and folks out late
crook-necked, a scared delight . . .

Not to see Halley's Comet . . .

# Witch heart
*(going to Robyn Archer's "A Star Is Torn")*

Driving tonight in freezing air
to cram the Comedy's windy foyer

we go to see a red bitch raise
eleven dead nobles from the grave

eleven ladies they had a ball
and a century to their funeral

oh they sang good and they lived hard
it was one-night stands on a dead-end road

and it's cold the gusts and black in the street
and hail comes across and peppers it white

and through the Comedy's blue and dark
we'll be those nobles screwed and starred

and raped and hurt and drunk and broke
and jailed and dead and young that ache

those ladies high in the wind and the rain
that lights them up and batters them down

one red-haired bitch talks down the years
eleven dead whores dress up their blues

the witch heart sings from a bloodless face
and lives the triumph of that distress

and the living and loving are women the more
all that festivity and power

# *Nasturtia!*

1978–1982

Whirligig

# A bed of nasturtiums

If she were to say,
twenty-two nasturtiums
I sowed in pairs,
just in case –
pity to chance a gap
in their heartening ranks;

if she were to say,
the twenty-two perking up
are my proof
something moves
inside the grid, different
from storm-force children;

she might be misunderstood,
her ragged show (late-flowering
Giant Red)
presenting
desirousness deep as an artery
opened, and afterwards

pale-lipped veiny and shrivelled,
finally not mattering.
Something else too,
the nous to
recur – pushy but by-the-way.
Which she'd find hard to say.

## Nasturtium grows

Nasturtium grows up in the night
till Dayleen peeps between the slats;
her third-floor possie in the flats
has things inside the proper height.
Things that keep going should be cut,
she knows. And pulls the white slats shut.


## Her lookout

Nasturtium peering through the glass
watches the rootless people pass
from pose to pace from room to roam
their dream of gardens. Stay-at-home
Nasturtium trampled in her place
wonders at the human race.

## Prophetic nasturtium

Nasturtium's little lamp shines red;
the great sun's representative,
all fire and fuel, I heard roar Live!
and hosts stirred in the garden bed.
As I write, it's gone rose, now pale,
now withered. Don't believe my tale.


## Epic nasturtium

Valiant and mighty is Nasturtium
that comes up shouldering clods to sit
it out like Troy, through vermin, shit
of dogs, contempt, drought and immersion;
then welcomes in the Hooves of slaughter –
two men laying pipes to spray the water.

# Emblem

Nasturtium is as Nasturtium does – me,
in bed I face her bed because she
flounces in the hedgerow gloom, wreathes
roots among clover, runs to bloom, breathes
garden breath through all her salady
greenery, and meditates no malady.

# Wanton

No sooner moved in on me, the ribald
mob in a second almost doubled;
I fiddled with Thrive – I needn't have troubled
for a rabble where greedy bees tippled and juggled;
now Nasturtium ramps all over the bed
and niggles the living and nibbles the dead.

## Nasturtium no student

Dons find this lowbrow lot, impervious
to the classic fount, just basks there greening;
frisks under sprinklers, droops at learning —
it can't take in a drop that's previous.
So not to countenance inertia,
"Nasturtiums!" bawls one. And one, "Nasturtia!"

## The rising generation

Family says Di should trim the rout
of bright young things, for known and valid
nasturtian uses — pickles, salad.
Unfazed, she approves its layabout
abandon on the tides of weed;
she finds it "gay". That's all they need.

## Nasturtium watches the cyclists

Stretching from prone, Nasturtium feels
that humans, stalked as tall as wheat,
should be content with having feet
instead of mounting them on wheels;
the ways things are, our reason's throne . . .
climbing to sun over the stone.

## Nasturtium untanned

Dayleen and Di get round like ghosts
in the rain, upset by fading suntan;
almost set back their dates at the unplanned
letdown — if anyone at the Coast
saw them! Nasturtium ogles sky
in twenty colours. She'll get by.

# Nasturtium regardless

Bumptious Nasturtium keeps on sending
bunches where no-one really wants her;
floods paths, bursts out in hedges, flaunts a
bud at each flamboyant ending.
Resistant to the strongest hint,
she cannot stop, she cannot stint.


# Her company

Nasturtium tangles with nutgrass, clover
and worse; such promiscuities
bring proper Dayleen on her knees
to give the weeds a going-over.
Eradicated, in a week
they're back there making free. What cheek!

# Showdown

Nasturtiums? no, these unsucked straws
left sticking up — stumps drying to thread —
mere stalks. Di rages, hunts the cause,
sprays. Now the leafless clumps turn dead
yellow. Last green to go, the killer
shows up, still-lusty Caterpillar.

# Viewing

Braving together autumn's flurries
to view a fresh nasturtial sprout:
"Baby," beams Di, "we made it out!"
"Not much going on there," Dayleen worries,
"I spose they'll all be your side, and
they'd better not get out of hand."

## Hardy Nasturtium

Nasturtium, reeling in a northwest
gale, divines the sense of cowering
southeast, and does, until the towering
stiff shrubs lie smashed and treetops roar less . . .
then straightens. Blasts the smart fool poohpoohs,
a prey to light variable schoolshoes.


## The confirmation

Nasturtium wavers towards conversion,
sighing after Rose-aeons of allusion –
paean, pun, screed, skit, fyt and effusion
all Rose. On high, the Great Nasturtium
invents, unfurls, revolves imposing
flame. The adoring border glows.

## Fat in winter

Thickening out in winter, Di
thinks forward to famishing and de-
hydration, baring stylishly
the new-baked flesh . . . but it's July.
Touch toes, and eat. Nasturtium's clump
spreads, gusts ply the big-leaved frump.

## The long hot summer

Nasturtium in disorder twigs
they've all moved on, even the young called
Get-off-that-bed! She's never sprinkled;
the border's going to the dogs;
at Surfers', oiled and dunked and eyed
and grilled, girls make for drinks and shade.

# No question

On mammals huge Nasturtium gazes
that on Nasturtium urinate,
none of them questioning how fate
purges, fulfils, corrodes, amazes
the quivering pup, the fainting stamen,
the fuming muck, the zip-up human.

# One and Many

Nasturtium's found philosophy
treats of the Many and the One;
her Andean generation
strut intercontinentally
the Sun's own suit (flammivomous rout!)
finessed (a chance nick drains the root).

# One night

Lights out, the boughs that crush and part
nearby, uneven grass in sog,
shuddered dog-contributions, flag-
ging vine, small fog, and stars in doubt –
the house-end's stark. The moon's sarcastic.
Nasturtium tarts up in yellow plastic.

# Nasturtium scanned

Ropey, lippy, loopy, scribbly
over a brick's edge, she's a riot,
straggly as random and tricky as a diet,
tiddly, wobbly, oddly nibbly
and flashy as a landmine on her vine-meandrine
Alexandrine tangle-scanned line.

and one more . . .

# Naming Nasturtium

Nasute *Tropaeolum majus*,
Carroty-bleb and Tender-jaundice,
Inca-bell, Indian Criss-cross-cress-face,
Humble-lobe, Edge-scum, Overgrow, Base Bess,
Butter-bright, Brazen-jane, Sweet-thorn, Oughtless,
Many-green, Scullery-cheer, Leafpenny, Largesse.

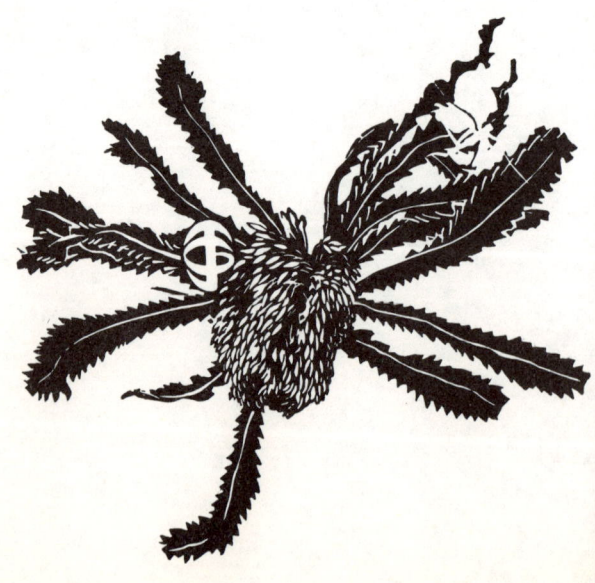